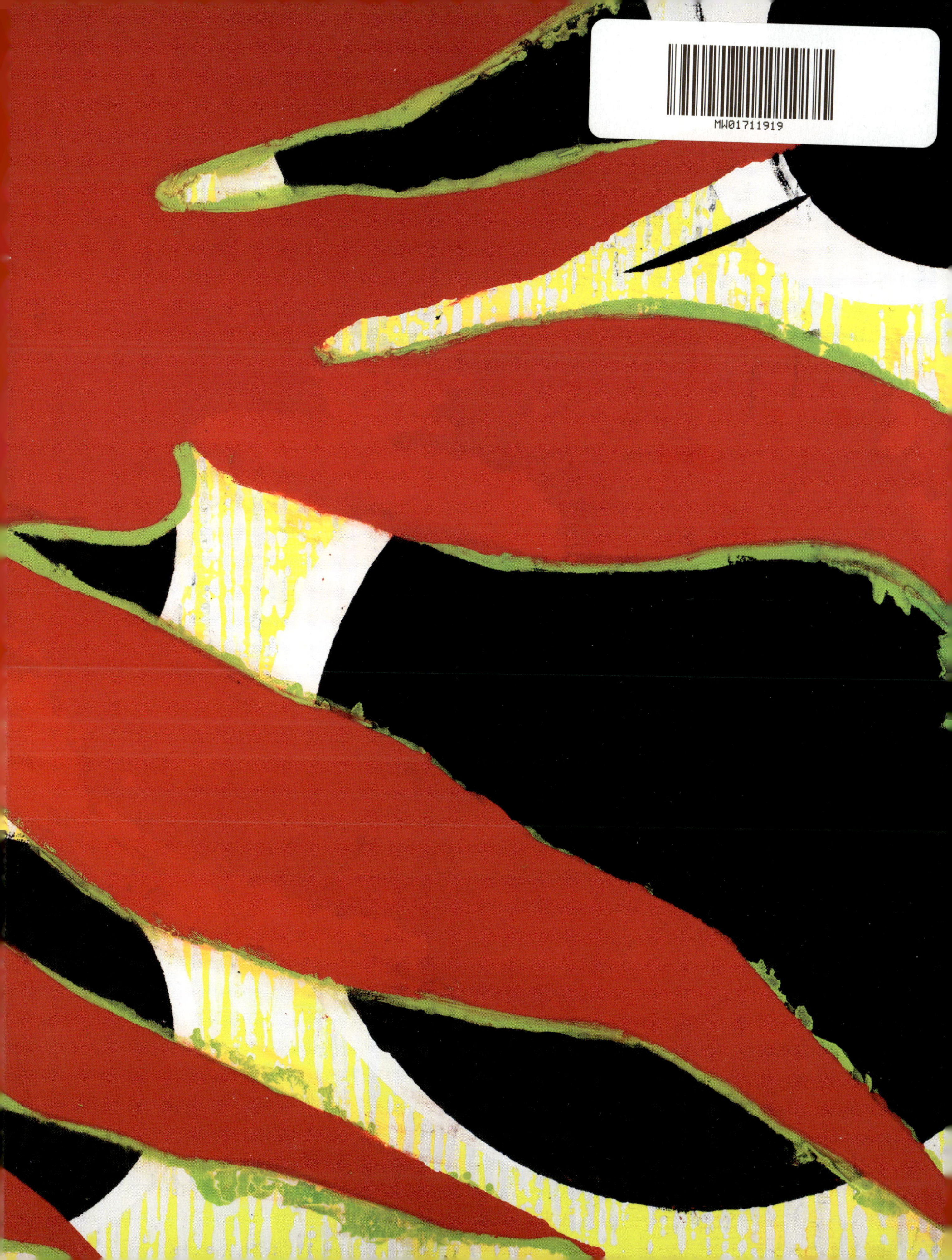

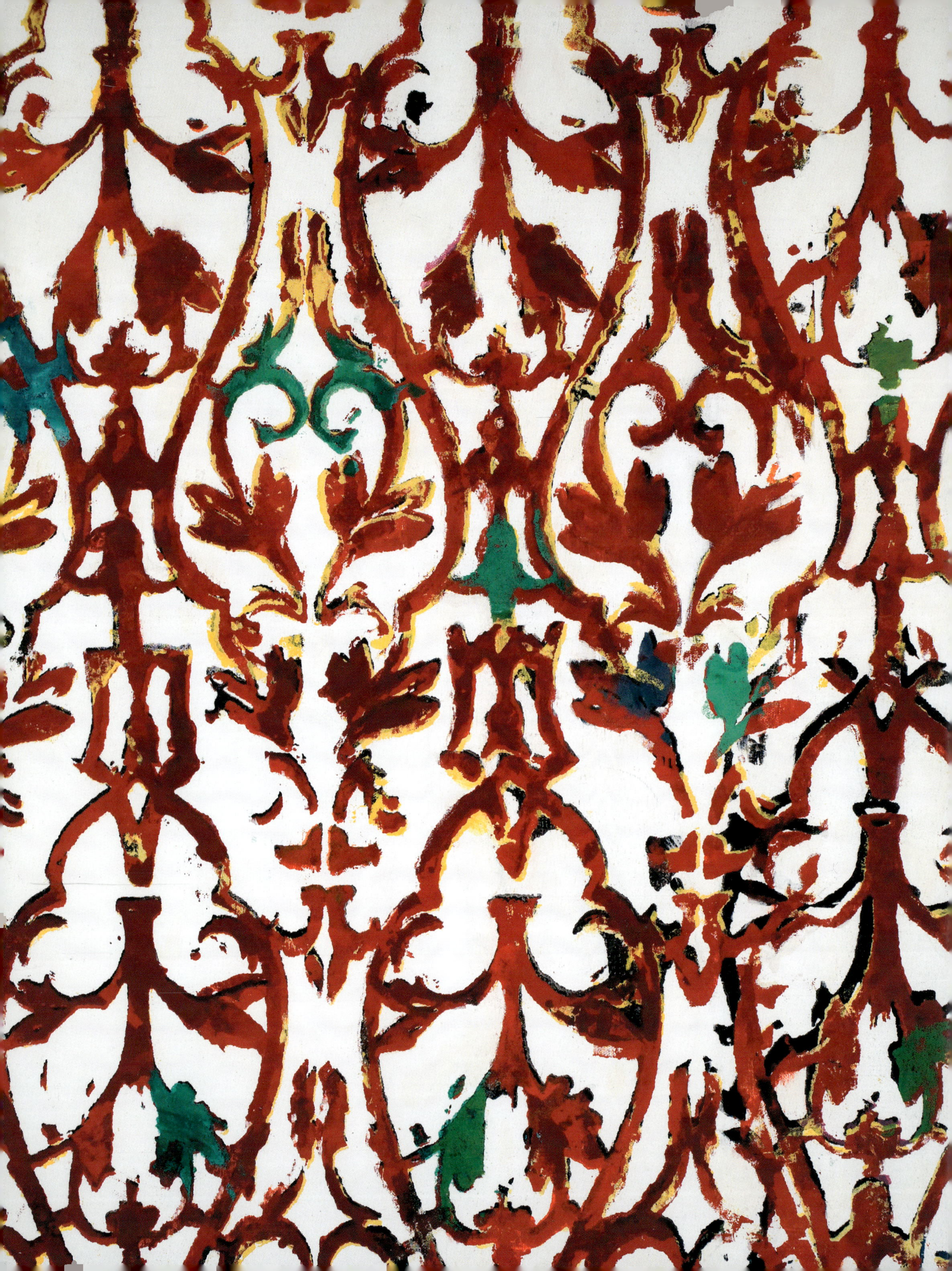

# MARGARET LANZETTA

# MARGARET

Iris and B. Gerald Cantor Art Gallery | College of the Holy Cross

# LANZETTA

## Pet the Pretty Tiger

WORKS 1990-2010

curated by Carol Schwarzman

essays by John Yau and Judy Halebsky

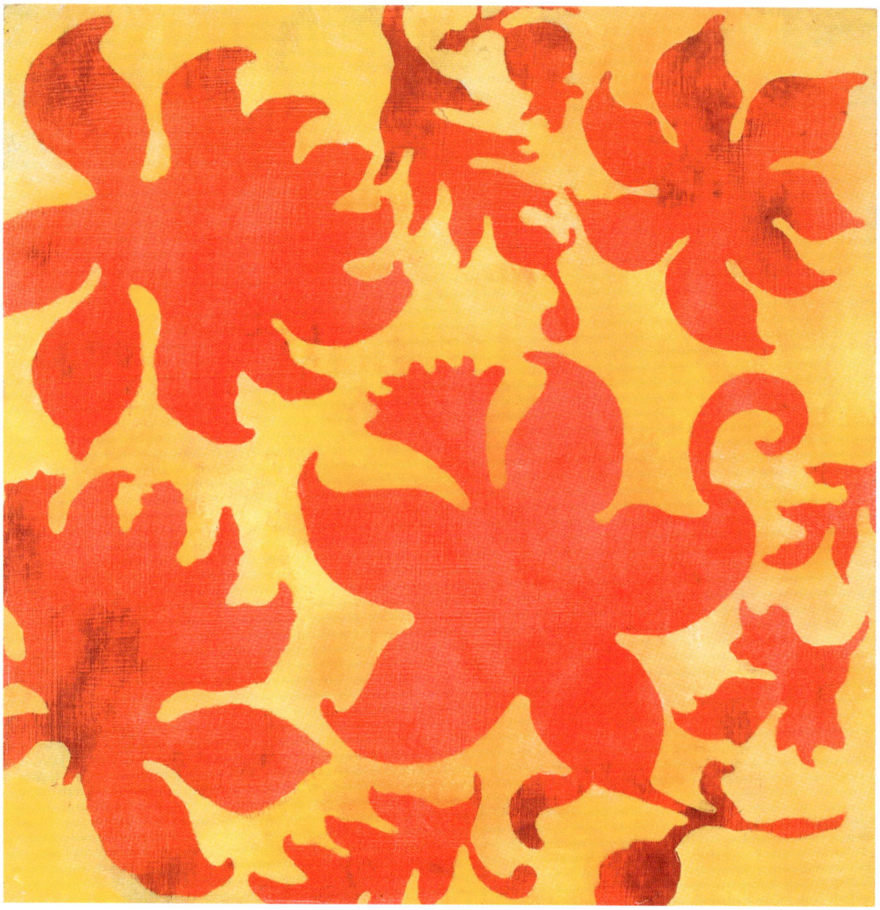

*above,* **Flirt**
2005
oil on panel
17" x 17"
Collection of Dan Cullen and Chris Welch, New York

*opposite,* **Long Sack/Collar**
1992
rubber and plastic cuff
120" x 7" diameter

*endpapers*
*detail:* **Across the Black Water**
2008
acrylic, enamel, and oil on panel
22" x 22"

*opposite half title*
detail: **Ambidextrous**
2004
oil, enamel, and acrylic on canvas
56" x 40 "

All photography by Kevin Noble unless as noted below:
Artist: cover, Bodakdev Road, Ahmedabad, India 2009, Pages 15, 17, 18, 20, 21, 22, 48, 50, 60 (Strangeness of Beauty), 66, 67, 70 (Bandgare), 73 (Echolalia N. 2), 80, 87, endpaper; (Artist's garden, summer); Jim Greene: page 33

Iris and B. Gerald Cantor Art Gallery
College of the Holy Cross
Worcester, Massachusetts 01610-2395
www.holycross.edu/cantorartgallery

ISBN: 978-0-9616183-5-3


*Book design by Chris Welch*
Exhibition title Pet the Pretty Tiger: from *The Invisible Dragon, Essays on Beauty* by Dave Hickey, 1993.

# CONTENTS



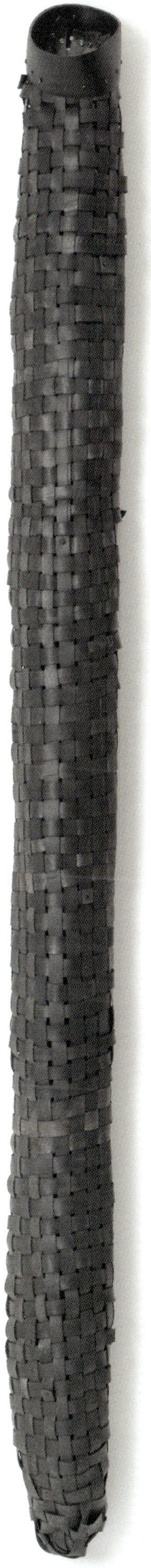

# FOREWORD

Margaret Lanzetta: Pet the Pretty Tiger: Works 1990 – 2010 at the Iris and B. Gerald Cantor Art Gallery is both an acknowledgement of a Holy Cross alumna's hard work and considerable success, and a survey of the work of a remarkable artist. Several years ago I was introduced to the vibrant and complex work that Margaret had been producing since the early 2000's. Later, I saw sculptures and paintings at her studio dating back 20 years or more, where germs of the later work had begun. Immediately, I hoped to organize a survey of her work at the gallery. This exhibition traces the trajectory of Margaret's substantial engagement in charting fresh territory in each series of sculptures, paintings and works on paper coupled with an astonishing array of first hand international cultural influences. Margaret lives and works in New York but has also spent various periods of time in Japan, Southeast Asia, Rome, Germany, India, Syria, or in artists' residencies such as the MacDowell Colony.

Margaret draws inspiration from many sources, but cites Buddhism, nature, Islamic architecture, industry and Sixty's pop culture as among the most significant. Reflecting further, she states that "nature as both inspiration and eclipser of culture is a persistent theme." The work incorporates "a complex amalgam of geometric forms and archetypal organic plant forms juxtaposed with repetitive patterns extracted from architecture and surface textures of industrial materials." Much gratitude goes to the keen curatorial efforts of Carol Schwarzman and the artist and to Judy Halebsky, Carol Schwarzman and John Yau for their insightful essays on Margaret's work over the years, reinforcing the depth and richness of the work and giving it the attention it deserves.

I thank Chris Welch for designing this beautiful catalogue and to Kevin Noble for his superb photographic services. Many thanks to Kenise Barnes and Leslie Gerber-Seid for their help in assembling work from private collections and to the many private and public lenders of work: Deborah Straussman, Assistant Registrar, the New York Public Library, Kenise Barnes, Pam Butler, Jody and Bill Gorin, Dawn and Chuck Hendricks, Jean-Yves Noblet, Bruce and Naomi Usher, Dan Cullen and Chris Welch, Susan Drew and Niall Worn. I thank the very capable Cantor Gallery staff, Paula Rosenblum, Timothy Johnson and Haley Allen '10 for their hard work on this exhibition. Lastly, I wish to thank Margaret for her considerable efforts and commitment of time and energy that made the exhibition and catalogue possible.

*Roger Hankins*
*Director, Iris and B. Gerald Cantor*
*Art Gallery*

*opposite,*
**White Sulphur**
2010
oil and enamel on panel
30" x 24"

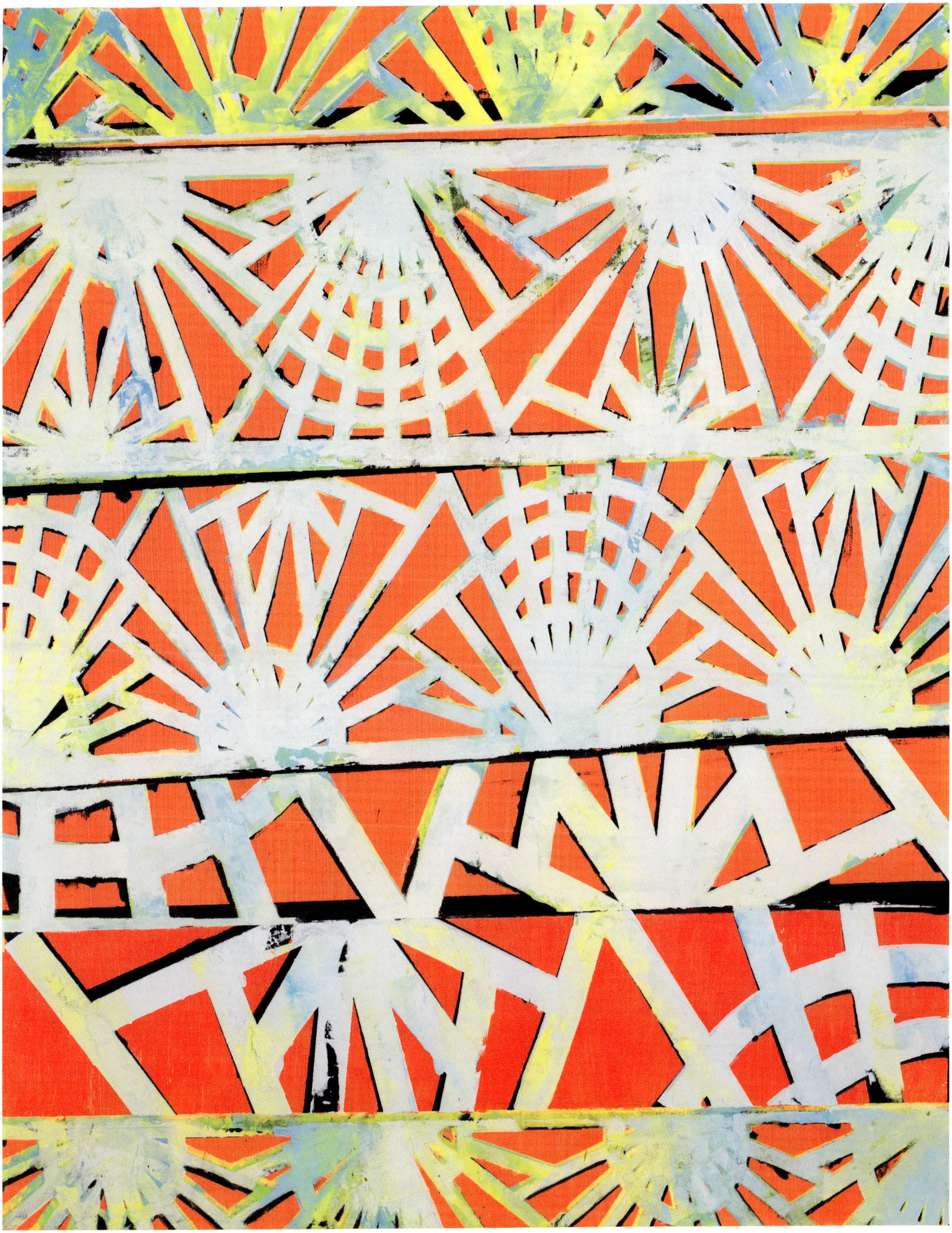

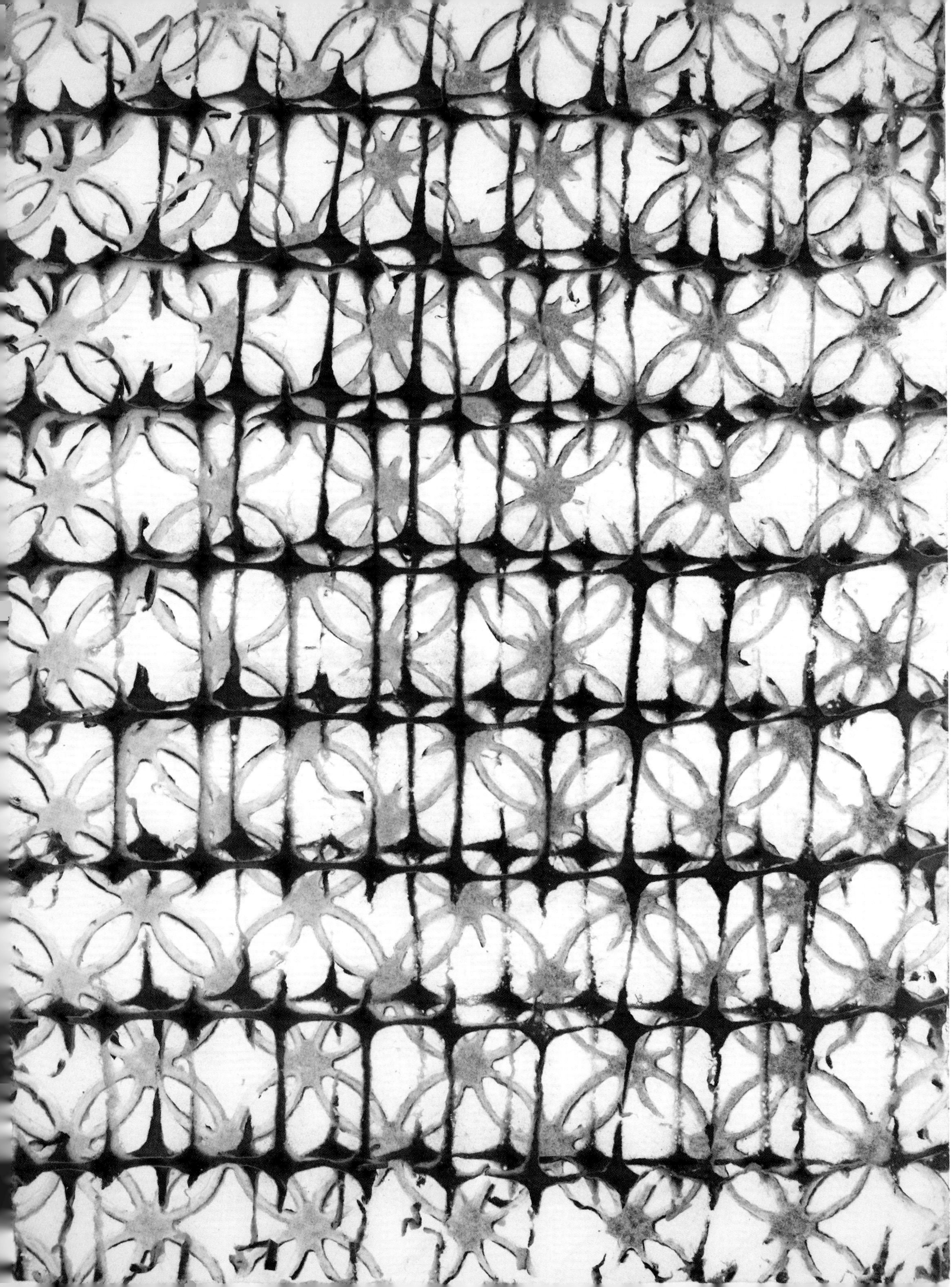

# INTRODUCTION

My association with Margaret began in the late '80s in New York, while we were attending the School of Visual Arts MFA program, back when she was using a circular saw to cut and build architectonic sculptures. Always in possession of an amazing, full-frontal, physical attack with materials—fearless and assured—Margaret tore through endless two-by-fours with a high-flying, inimitable energy. That physicality has been refined but not allowed to mellow in the paintings and prints selected for this current exhibition: vigorous, sensitive and verging on raw, the tensions and contradictions in these works are what make the viewing alternately pleasing and challenging. Yet let it be known that neither Margaret nor her work is about equivocation. Straddling oppositions, however, are a favorite area of her inquiry, as the title of this exhibit suggests.

Pleasure, Beauty and Desire are always in the forefront of Margaret's concerns, as are the universality of decoration and pattern, issues of mechanical reproduction and our relationship with the natural world. Her postmodern romanticism forms a hybrid of industry and nature by initiating a site to fabricate at their intersection. Just look at her titles (which she spends much time revising and reconsidering) and their relationship to words and the self: she bridges the gap between image and language beautifully with *Eternity in an Hour* (citing William Blake) and *Glass Bead Game* (referencing Hermann Hesse's *Bildungsroman*). That these lyrical titles accompany imprints from cast off packaging materials or the detritus of large scale fabrication of consumer items launches them into the wide interstice between idealism and hope, on the one hand, and a resolute acceptance of reality on the other. Margaret's work seems to narrow that gaping space of indeterminacy— as if to give the viewer a way through considering the predicament of existence as a natural being in a sacred environment, while acknowledging an increasingly manmade world. An ardent urban gardener for many years, she has also spent hours crisscrossing the city with her camera, documenting the pervasiveness and persistence of plant life throughout the concrete landscape.

Over the years, she has mentioned Yayoi Kusama and Andy Warhol as two artists she looks to for inspiration. The sculptors Allan McCollum and Jackie Winsor also come to mind as influences: McCollum because of his immersion in issues of beauty and reproduction through endless variation and the infinite (ditto Kusama) and Winsor because of a formal physicality that ranges from raw to elegant in the service of a series. Thinking of Margaret's work in terms of sculpture makes sense because both her paintings and prints never

**Glass Bead Game**
1998-99
screenprinted paper pulp
on cotton rag
30" x 22"
Collection of Susan
Drew, Los Angeles

really offer an invitation into an illusionistic space. Instead, they strive to make the viewer aware of her/himself in relation to a physical vibration of pattern, color and imagery. Her connection to Warhol, and through him to Duchamp, comes by way of her nomination of everyday sources as the basis on which to build her compositions. Lacking the flippancy to be deadpan, the ironies in her work may borrow from Pop sources, but ultimately they lead us to consider the quotidian and its rhythms as a foundation for immanence.

*Pet the Pretty Tiger* is the first time many of these works have been seen together in one venue, offering the viewer an important opportunity to experience in-depth the rich dialogue the grouping creates. For the honor and pleasure of my involvement in bringing this occasion to the public, and on Margaret's behalf, many thanks go to gallery director Roger Hankins, the Iris and B. Gerald Cantor Art Gallery and the College of the Holy Cross for supporting this thought-provoking exhibition.

*Carol Schwarzman*
*Brisbane, Australia 2010*

*Carol Schwarzman is a visual artist and writer based in Brisbane, Australia and New York. Her solo exhibition,* Aerial View: Maps / Clouds / Thinking, *opened at PS Gallery, Brisbane in September 2010. Her recent articles on the Asia-Pacific Triennial and The ARC Biennial, both based in Brisbane, are featured in upcoming issues of Sculpture and Artlink magazines.*

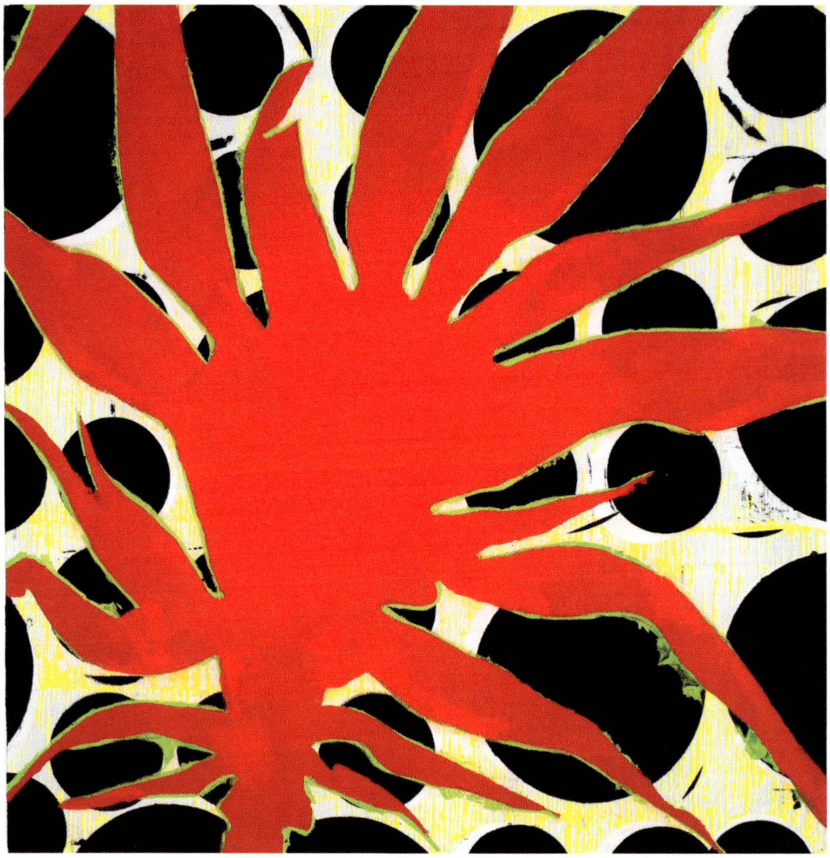

**Across the Black Water**
2008
acrylic, enamel, and oil on panel, 22" x 22"

*opposite,* **Eternity in an Hour**
2002
oil, enamel on panel, 18" x 18"
Collection of Dawn and Chuck Hendricks, New York

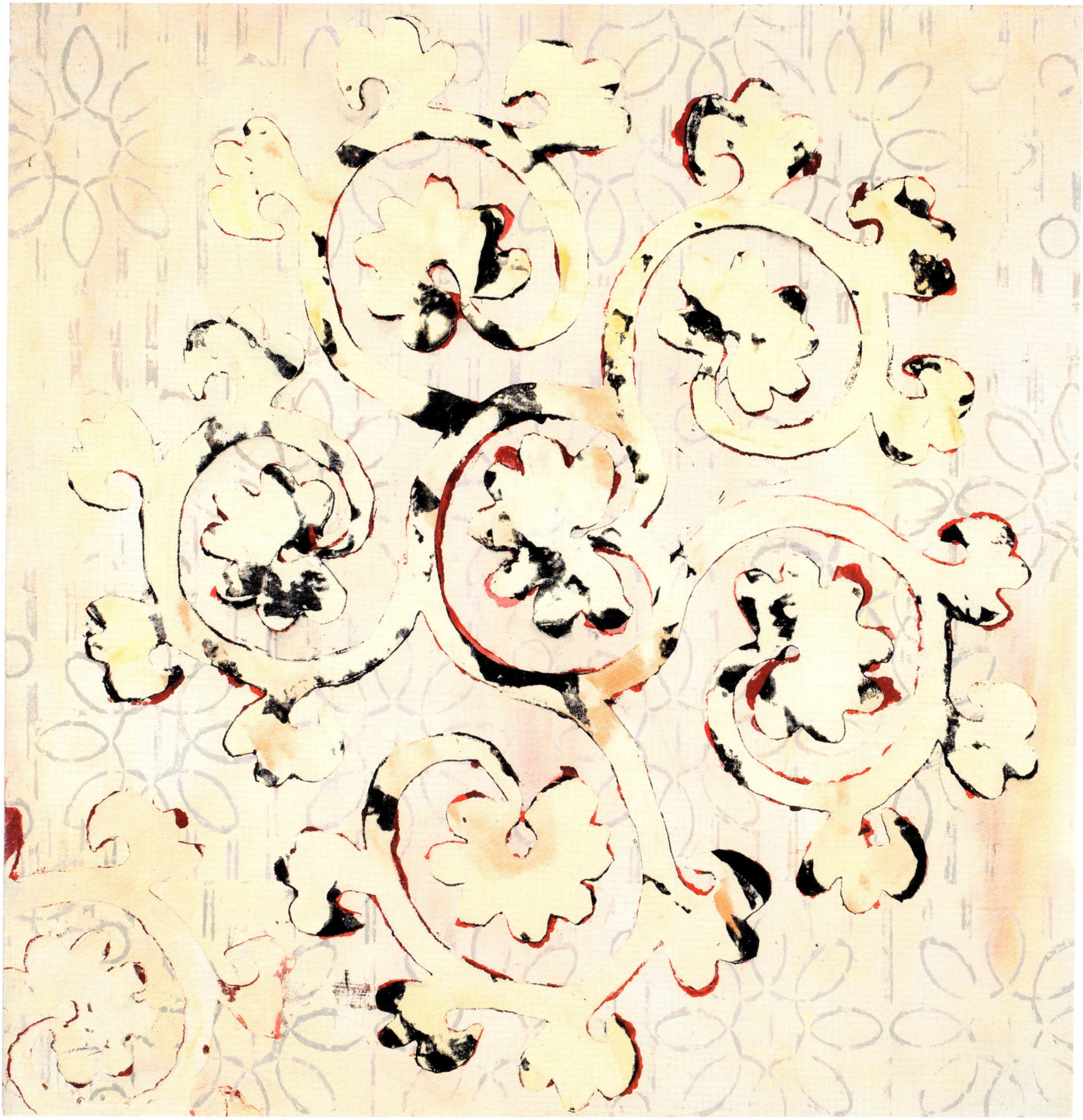

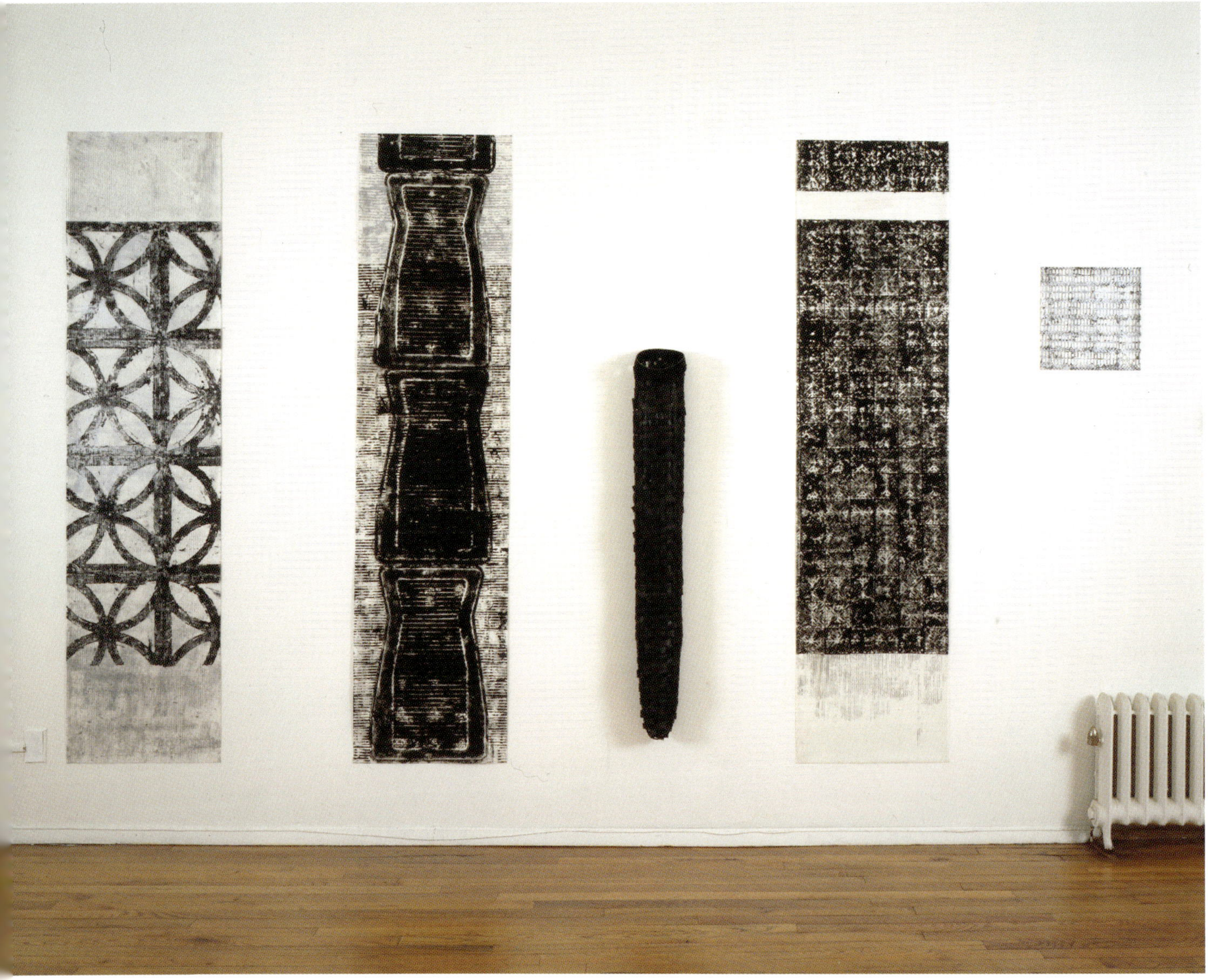

Artist's studio, West Third Street, New York 1993. *(from left to right):*

**Syncopation**

1993, acrylic and polyurethane on mylar, 84" x 21"

**Delivery**

1993, acrylic and polyurethane on mylar, 84" x 21" Collection of Museum of Modern Art, New York

**Short Sack/Collar**

1991, rubber and plastic cuff, 50" x 7" diameter

**Black Snow**

1993, acrylic and polyurethane on mylar, 84" x 21"

**Tracery**

1991, acrylic and polyurethane on mylar, 14" x 14"

# A POSTMODERN GARDEN

If the world exists to end up in a book, as the symbolist poet Stéphane Mallarmé claimed, or as a bodiless image on a high resolution screen, as postmodernist theorists have advanced, then one of the artist's preoccupations is how to read and understand a constantly changing, visually insistent, multitudinous world. In Margaret Lanzetta's bold, graphic paintings, the artist weaves, jams together and recombines patterns and shadow images in order to understand their often-unacknowledged presence in our lives. We see them, but do not notice them. Derived from both the world she inhabits and the very different societies in which she has traveled and stayed for extended periods of time— Japan, India, Syria, etc— her vocabulary of silhouettes and symbolic motifs embraces the postmodern age and ancient cultures, both East and West. Her sources encompass Buddhism and stylized details of Islamic architecture; nature (plant forms) and machinery (gear wheels and cogs); ordered and disordered grids; patterns and repetitions of distinct organic or geometric structures; and abstract, decorative signs often rendered in industrial or printer's saturated colors. Out of this plethora of diverse and competing languages, many of which are embedded so deeply in their respective cultures as to be taken for granted, Lanzetta fashions both a response and a commentary.

In some of the earliest works in this two decade survey exhibition (1990-2010), Lanzetta has woven rubber strips into elongated containers that are simultaneously organic and machine-like. Her weaving, wrapping or nonmechanical repetition of industrial materials in sculptures such as *Arcanta Group* (1991) and *Long Sack/Collar* (1990) connects her to the pioneering sculptor Eva Hesse (1936-1970), who led the way from Minimalism to Postminimalism. In Lanzetta's case, it's as if she wanted to gather things together, or repair things, as the act of wrapping implies, as well as make a vessel-like form that could hold different elements. Working primarily as a sculptor in the late 1980s and early 1990s, the artist began

**Glassblower II**
2004
acrylic and pigmented pulp on paper
24" x 36 "

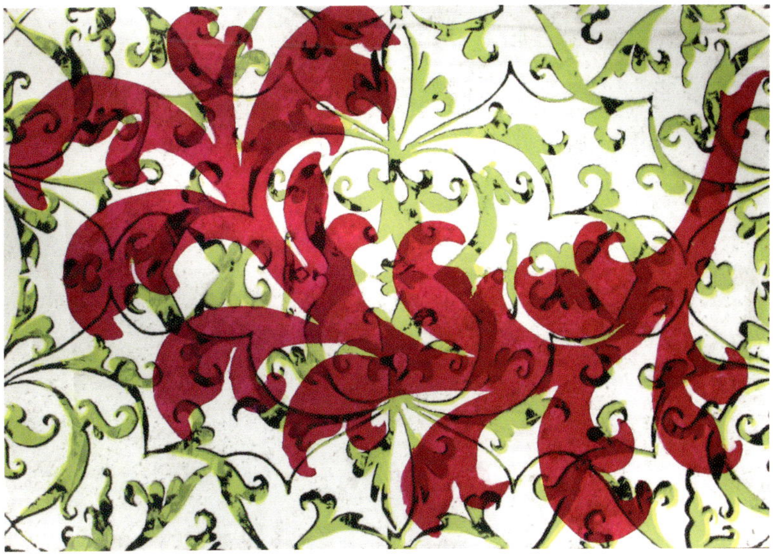

moving from the three dimensional realm to the two dimensional realm around 1992 without sacrificing her involvement with physically repetitive, meditative processes such as stacking, layering and weaving. One of the impulses that prompted this development was Lanzetta's strong desire to directly record physical imprints of the material world from which the sculptures emerged. To join the mechanical and organic in more extensive and meaningful ways, her insistent sculptural processes were transformed into stamping, rubbing and printing, first on seven foot and later ten foot long industrial Mylar panels that referenced not only the vertical scale of her sculptures, but also that of the human body. In *Delivery* (1993) and *Syncopation* (1994), two early paintings on Mylar, her vocabulary is effectively broadened with a more diverse range of materials and painting techniques. Materially, the use of rubber and Mylar prefigured concerns still central in Lanzetta's work: specifically the intersection of nature and industry. Rubber, a natural substance transformed through galvanization, still retains the sheen and texture of animal hides, while the translucency of Mylar, a manufactured plastic, recalls fine calfskin vellum.

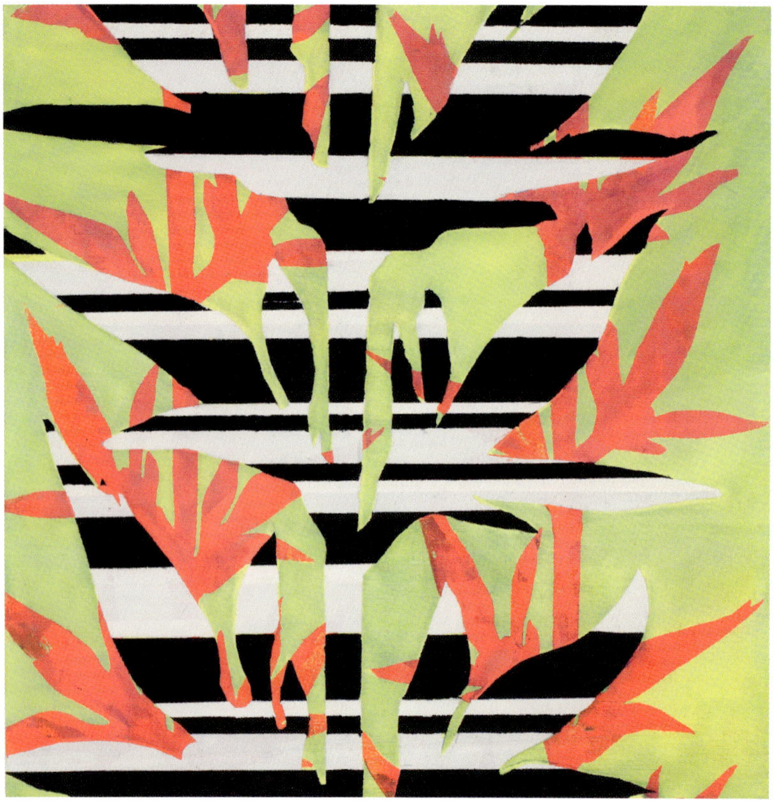

**Ballary 0839**
2009
oil and enamel on panel
24" x 24"

By combining a vocabulary derived from machine parts and surface textures of steel plates with floral patterns and architectural ornamentation, a grittiness emerges. It is as if modern technology and its often-deleterious effects have invaded paradise, which the floral patterns certainly recall. This is underscored through the forms she incorporates, as well as her use of intense, saturated color. The dark lotus floating near the center of *Lotus (cayenne)* (2005-06), for example, seems on some level to have succumbed to the effects of a poisonous world, while the overlay of rich black, flower-like machine parts in *Signal Jumping, Black* (2010) or *It's All Spiritual* (2010) transform the decorative into something far-removed from paradise.

At the same time, recognizing that mutation is constantly pressuring and altering forms, particularly those that have migrated across different cultures and historical periods, the artist deploys a variety of means to transfer her vocabulary from one domain to another; including silkscreen, digital technology, traditional oil paint, enamel, acrylic, and even pigmented pulp as in the *Brittle Spring* series (1998-1999),

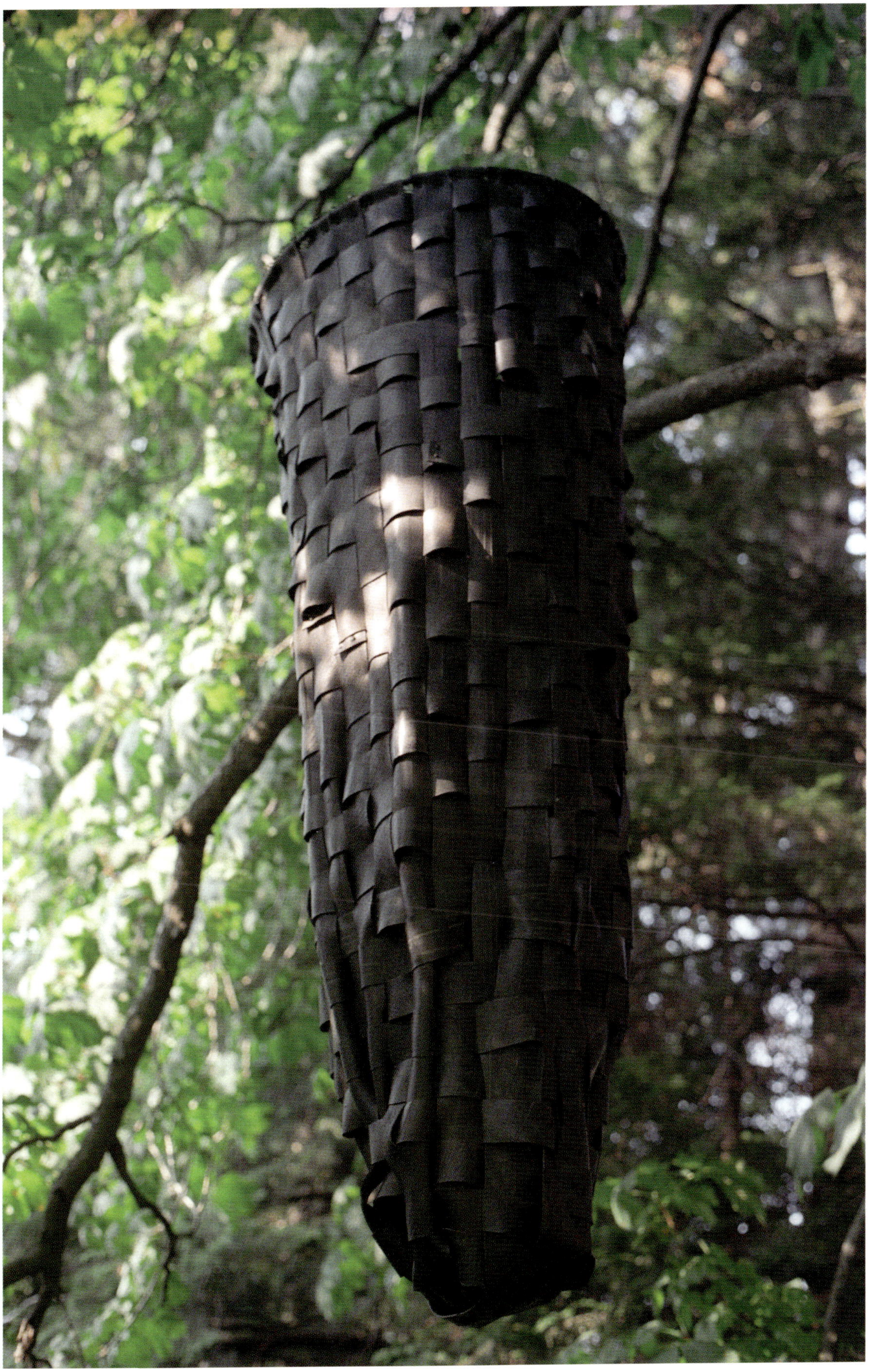

**Arcanta Group**
1991
rubber and steel, site specific installation at Chesterwood, Massachusetts
five units, each 72" x 24" diameter

*opposite,*
**Howrah 0322**
2009
oil and enamel on panel
24" x 24"

*below,* ***Company Paintings*** series,
Artist's studio, Long Island City 2010

a suite of unique pulp paintings created during a Workspace Residency Grant at the Dieu Donne Papermill. Through these mechanical means of reproduction, combined with hands-on, textural applications of paint, the artist underscores the extent to which industrialization and postmodern technology have become pervasive influences on our environment and the way we view it. She acknowledges that we live in a world of media-images, enmeshed in relentless fields of visual information. Thus a question I believe the artist poses to the viewer as well as herself is whether mechanical repetition means the destruction of things done by hand or can the two be made to coexist constructively? There is a sense that the artist believes coexistence can occur, but recognizes that this may not always happen.

Over the past twenty years, Lanzetta has gathered together a diverse vocabulary that enables her to construct multilayered works that evoke a host of narratives, none of which can be reduced to an overriding story. By this, I do not mean to imply that certain themes and preoccupations aren't evident, because that isn't the case. One constant theme reappearing is the sharp collision between the natural world and cultural production, with the understanding that humans have invested far too much belief in the artificial. Another theme, as previously advanced, is the conflict between modern technological advances and ancient traditions.

By enlarging and transforming flowers into bodiless silhouettes and placing them against a patterned background, as she does in series such as *Cultural Instructions* (2001-2004) and

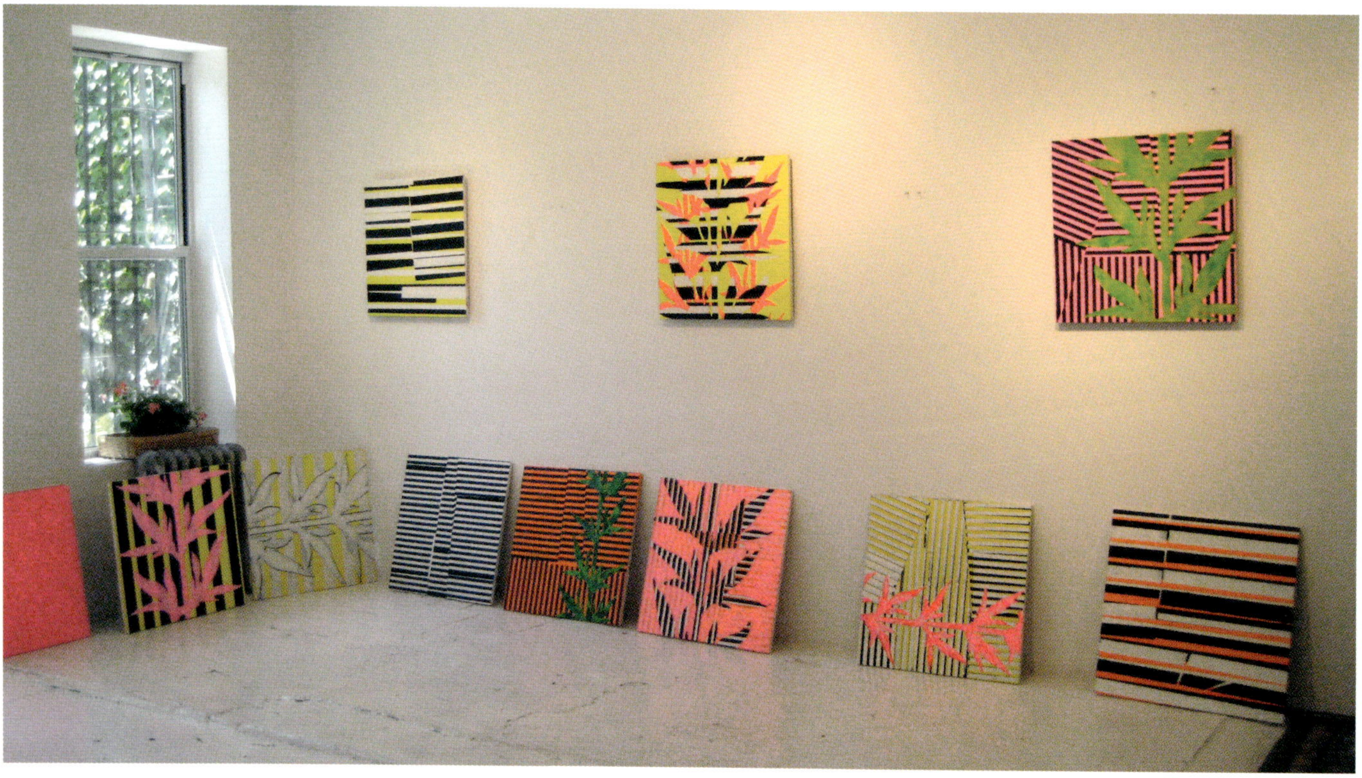

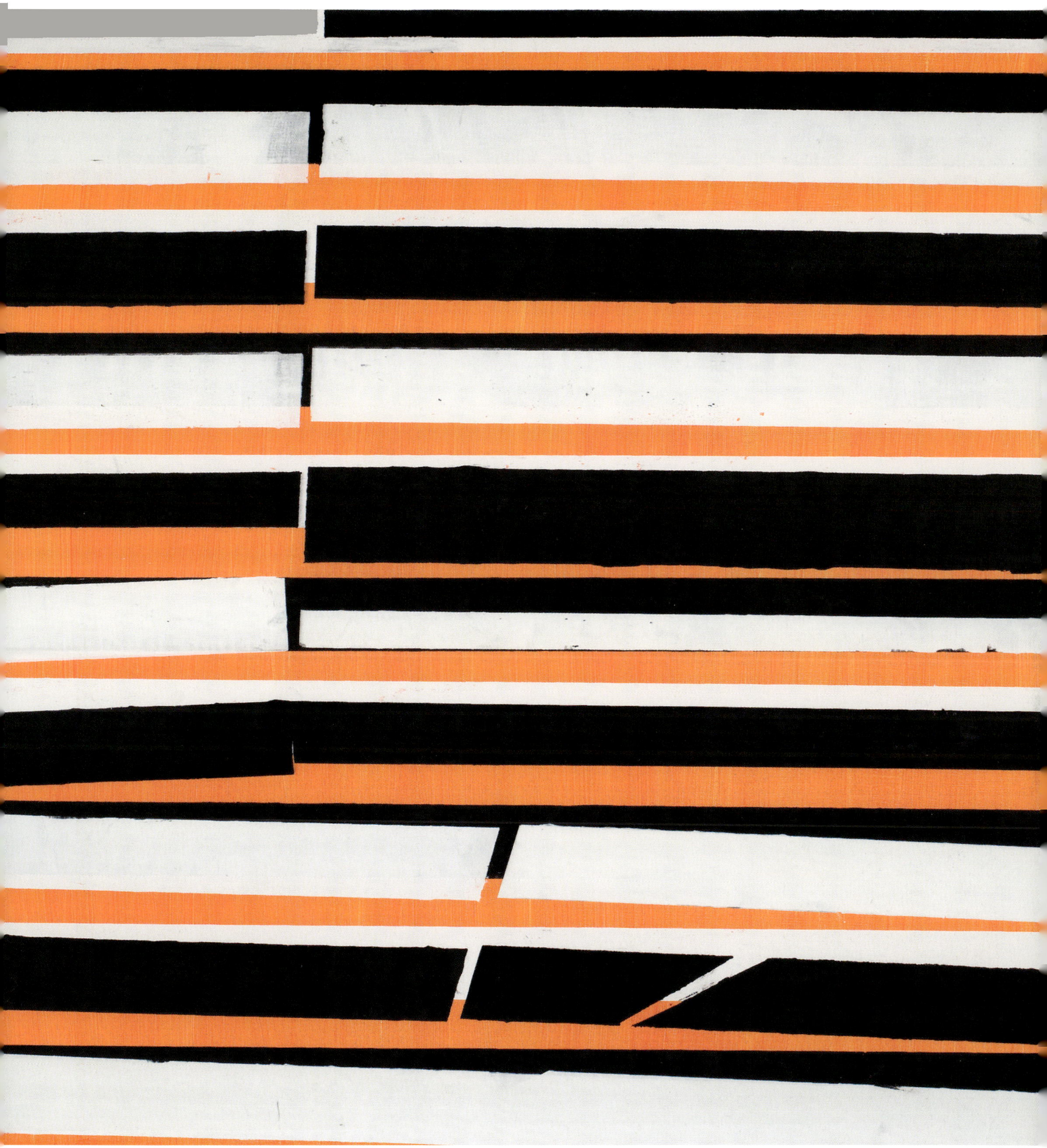

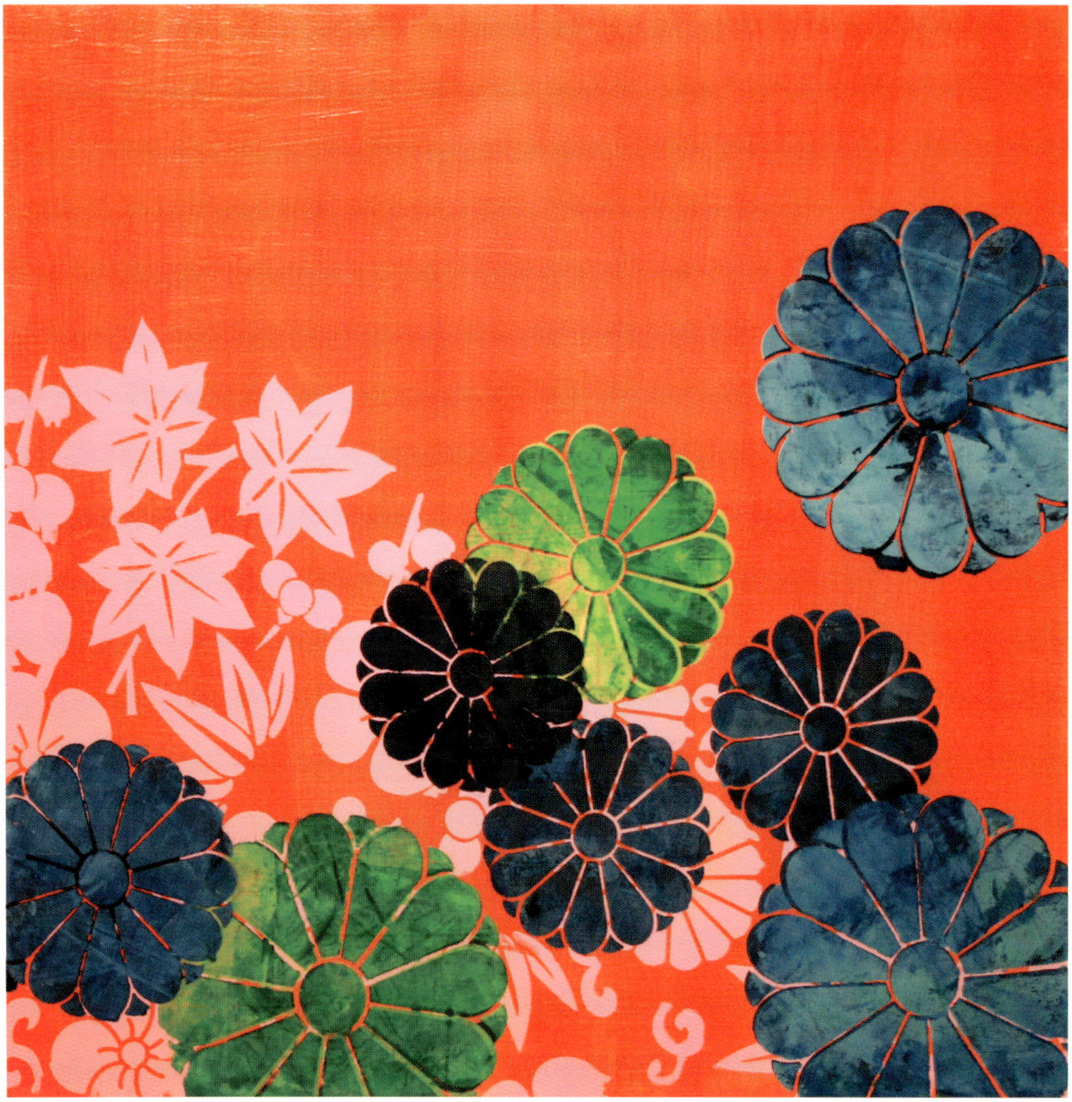

**Lotus (cayenne)**
2007
oil and enamel on panel
21" x 21"
Collection of Leslie and
Michael Meyers, New York

*Company Paintings* (2009), Lanzetta evokes the history of wallpaper as an inexpensive substitute for paintings; still-life paintings; the changing reality we inhabit, where plant life itself is becoming altered; black-and-white noir films of the forties and fifties, particularly those influenced by German Expressionism with their fondness for exaggerated lighting and elongated shadows; and the lingering effects of colonialism and unregulated industrialization on rural culture.

Conceived and completed after the artist's six month Fulbright Research Fellowship to India and Syria in 2008, the *Company Paintings* series (2009) consists of twelve paintings in square format. Using a vocabulary of alternating bands and one plant motif, Lanzetta limited herself to using four silkscreens printed in different color combinations. Each painting is titled the name and telephone area code of a remote Indian town, such as *Beed 0442*. According to the artist, the title for the series "comes

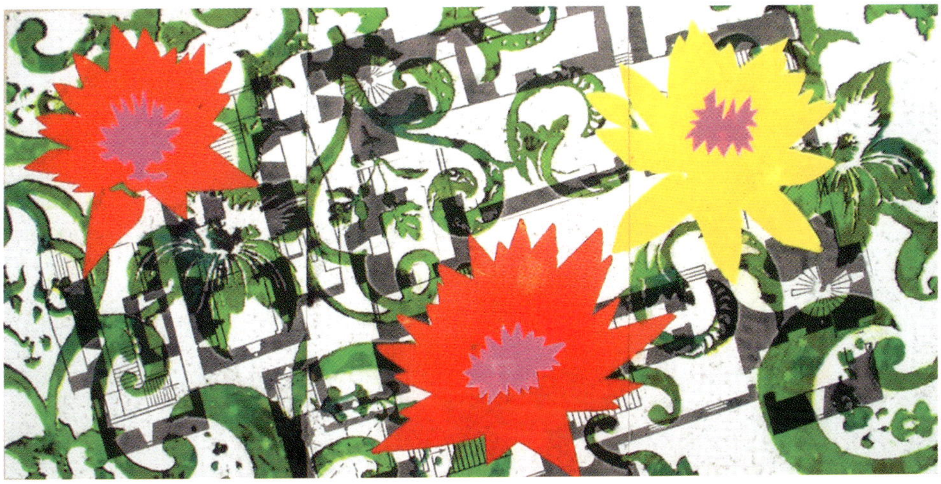

**Lilypad Deployment I**
2006
enamel, acrylic, digital ink, and mixed media on canvas mounted on panel
14" x 36"
Private Collection, New York

from the term for works commissioned by the East India Company to document India in the middle of the 18th century." A British corporation, originally chartered during the reign of Queen Elizabeth I, the East India Company monopolized trade between England and India for more than one hundred years; the commissioned paintings were meant to present the rosier side of colonialist history.

Lanzetta's *Company Paintings* are stark and jarring, their artificial colors hard and often disorienting. The series can be divided into three groups: those that juxtapose a plant form against geometric bands; those that create the plant form outline using geometric bands, thus inverting the figure-ground relationship; and those only made up of different colored bands, horizontally stacked. By working with a limited number of silkscreens, the artist is able to discover unlikely combinations, as well as push herself into new territory.

In *Howrah 0322*, the orange, black and white bands diminish in size as they rise toward the top edge, suggesting an aerial perspective of a landscape of tilled fields, as well as an unstable image found on old-fashioned television sets. By evoking these diverse readings, the artist underscores the ongoing clash between modern technology and ancient traditions that pervade many non-Western cultures, without offering a clear resolution to a persistent problem.

In *Jorhat 0376*, the artist juxtaposes a yellowish-green silhouette of an oversized plant against a pattern of vertical, horizontal and diagonal pink and black bands. There is something disturbing and threatening about the combination of forms and colors, which initially might come across as a still life, generally a benign subject, but upon further reflection clearly is not. The plant extends beyond both the top and bottom edge, disorientating a sense of its actual size; the leaves seem too large, as if the plant has been feeding on hormones. For all their repetition, the pink and black bands lack a detectable order. Why are some bands diagonal and others horizontal?

Questions like these, which are addressed directly to what the viewer sees, lead to other questions. What initially seems like a familiar image becomes less so the longer we look. In

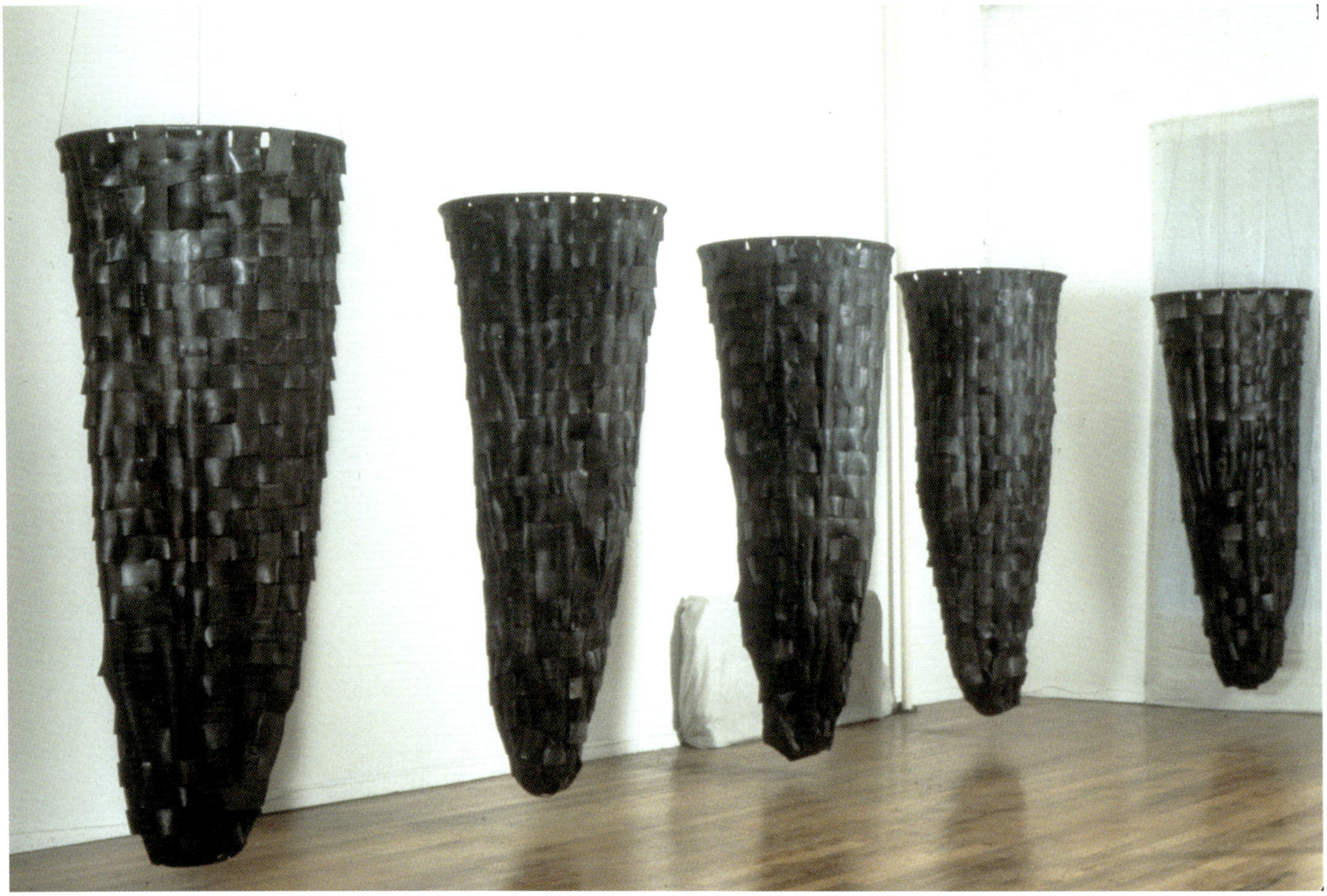

Artist's studio,
West Third Street, New York
**Arcanta Group**
1991 rubber and steel
five units, each 72" x 24" diameter

*opposite,*
**Transfer Effect**
2010
acrylic on paper
36" x 26"

*Jorhat 0376* and other paintings, such as *Biophilia Eve* (2007) and *Last Two Million* (2008), a spiky flower or benign houseplant becomes super-sized and menacing. I would characterize this as one of Lanzetta's strengths— she can turn a familiar image strange, as well as transform what is perceived as elegant and decorative into something cold and threatening. This even persists, as with *Howrah 0322*, when the artist restricts herself to repeating geometric patterns. Again, in *Karnal 0184*, only horizontal bands of yellow, black and white are used. However, some bands are tilted, while a vertical band interrupts others, causing symmetry and asymmetry to collide. Order, it seems, has broken down, and disruption is unavoidable.

In *Ballary 0839*, the combination of plant-like shapes and geometric bands is pushed to an extreme, making it difficult to distinguish figure from ground. If anything, they keep exchanging roles: in one view we might conclude that the leaf-like shapes defined by black and white bands are in front of the yellowish-green leaf-like shapes filled with reddish-magenta leaf-like shapes. However, this view reverses, and we can also believe that the yellowish-green leaf-like shapes are in front of the black and white bands. The instability of the view

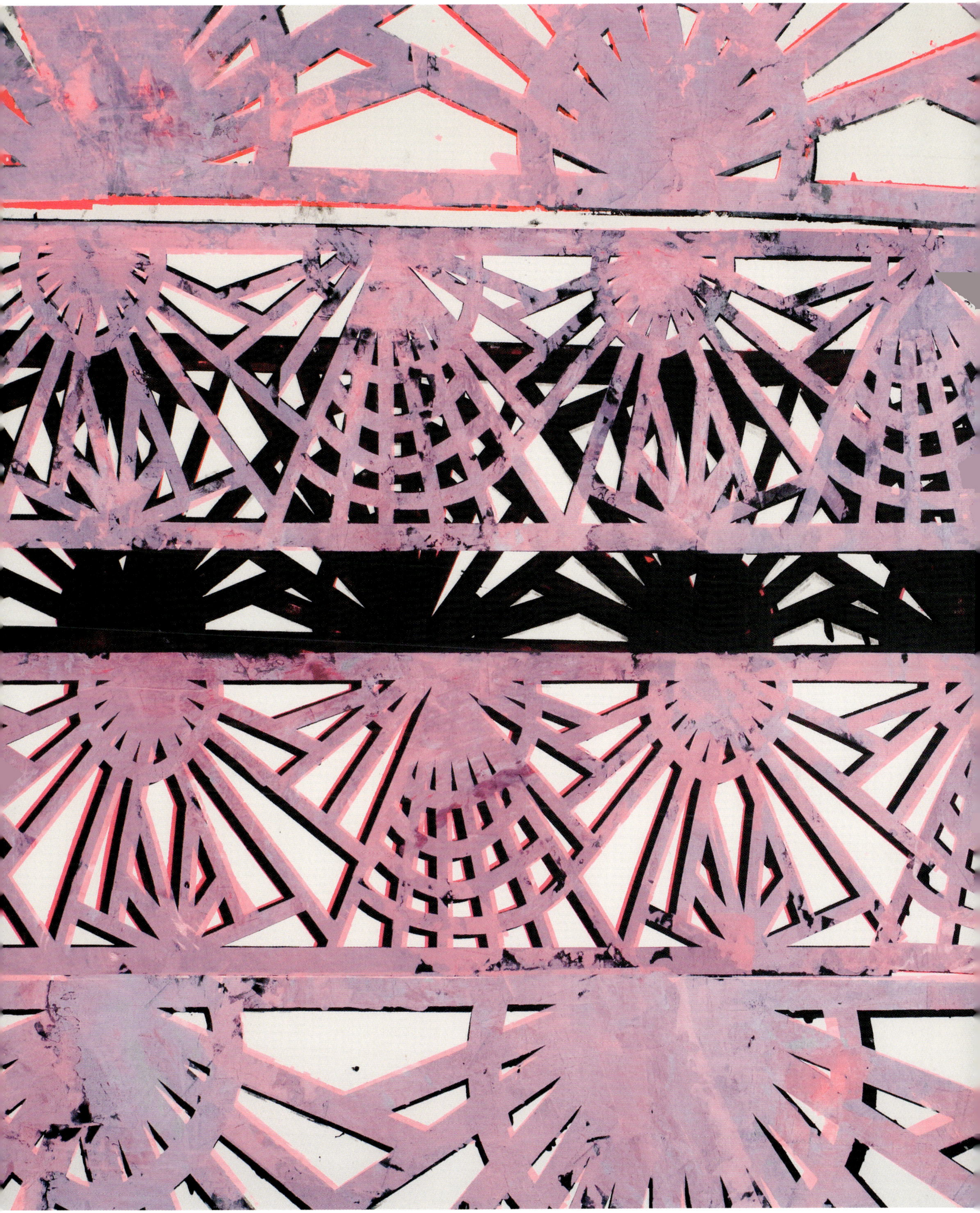

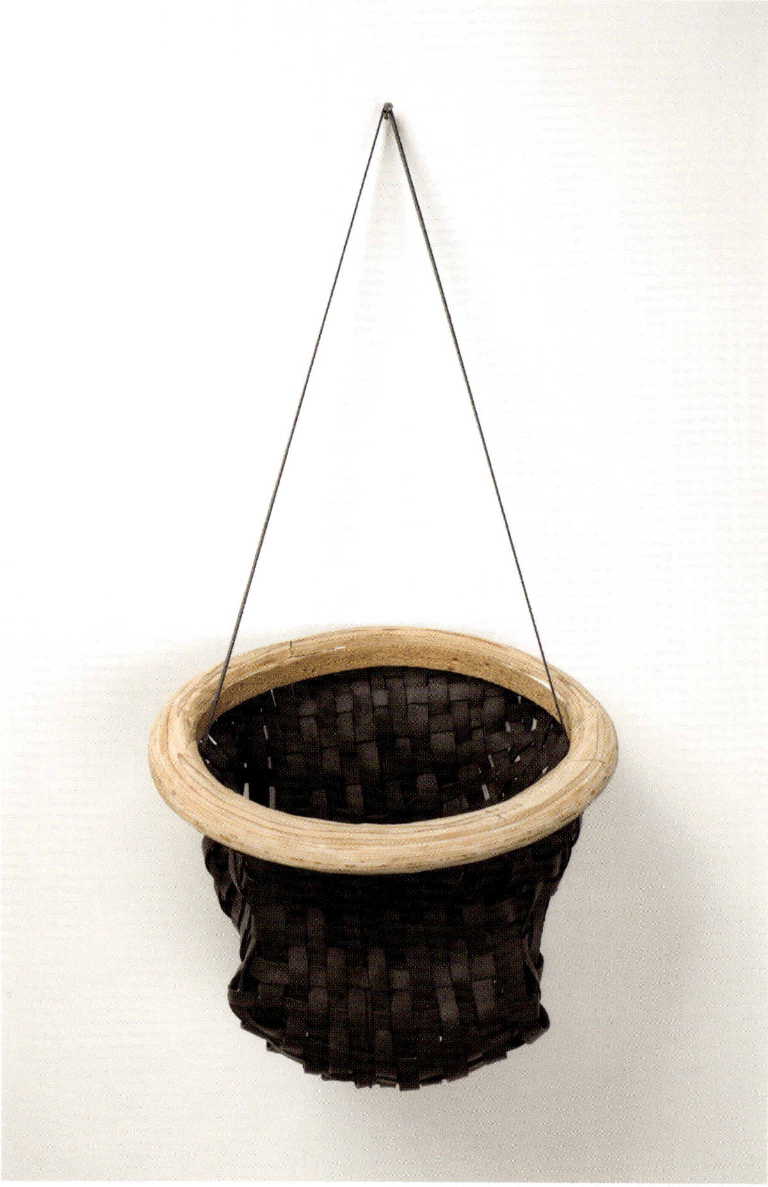

**Popotoafd**
1990
rubber and wood
28" x 14" diameter

becomes a comment on the subject—the inextricable embrace of form and content is troubling. In contrast to Bridget Riley and other artists involved with op art, Lanzetta recognizes that there is no pure state of seeing; everything is inflected by culture and history.

The clash between symmetry and asymmetry, order and disorder, underscores Lanzetta's vision of reality as a struggle between two opposing forces made of the same, if not identical, stuff. In this sense, the artist undermines the sense of order and decorum normally associated with decorative and architectural patterns. She reminds us that the world has gone awry, and that there is no clear agreement on a resolution. We can neither restore the old order, nor determine how to create a new, widely beneficial order. Even the idea of progress is called into question.

Conflict, entropy, mutation are also not concepts we think of with regard to floral patterns or decorative motifs. Yet that is precisely what the viewer encounters in Lanzetta's work. In the *Confection Series* (2005-06), which "relates to the proposed deployment of US military bases, dubbed 'lily pads', throughout Central Asia and North Africa," the artist mutates a lotus flower into exploding, cartoon-like forms, knowing that in actuality it grows in muddy water and rises above the surface to bloom, thus signifying in Buddhism rebirth and the purity of heart and mind. Clearly, another preoccupation of the artist is the devaluation of language and symbols. By transforming the lotus into an exploding form, the artist comments not only on external events over which she has no real control, but she also frames the viewer's relationship to art.

In *Lilypad Deployment I*, (2006) jagged orange and yellow forms float above a stylized floral motif and an aerial view of a plan for an enclosed fortress. In *Glassblower II*, (2005), part of the *Recitativo Series*, a large, elegant magenta floral form stretches across a ground of yellow arabesques. Its translucency evokes both the glassblower's breath and the fantastic shapes that molten glass can assume. Is art meant to be something pretty— a lush floral pattern, for example? Or can art insinuate itself into our lives, make us more aware of the world we inhabit? Rather than answering this question, and thus becoming ideological, the artist leaves it up to the viewer to decide what role art will play in her or his life.

Art, Lanzetta's work advances, can offer many possibilities, as well as lead to many places. Her work of the past two decades is the record of a journey and a search, as well as a document of one's passing through time and history. For all of its subjectivity, the work is neither inward and personal nor purely political. Rather, there is an openness to her work, motivated by an attempt to embrace the myriad networks and patterns of information saturating the contemporary world.

*John Yau*
*New York 2010*

*John Yau is a poet and critic living in New York. His latest book is A Thing Among Things: The Art of Jasper Johns (DAP, Distributed Art Publishers, 2008). He has just completed a book, Glamourless Reality, which will be published in 2011 and is an Associate Professor at Mason Gross School of the Arts (Rutgers University).*

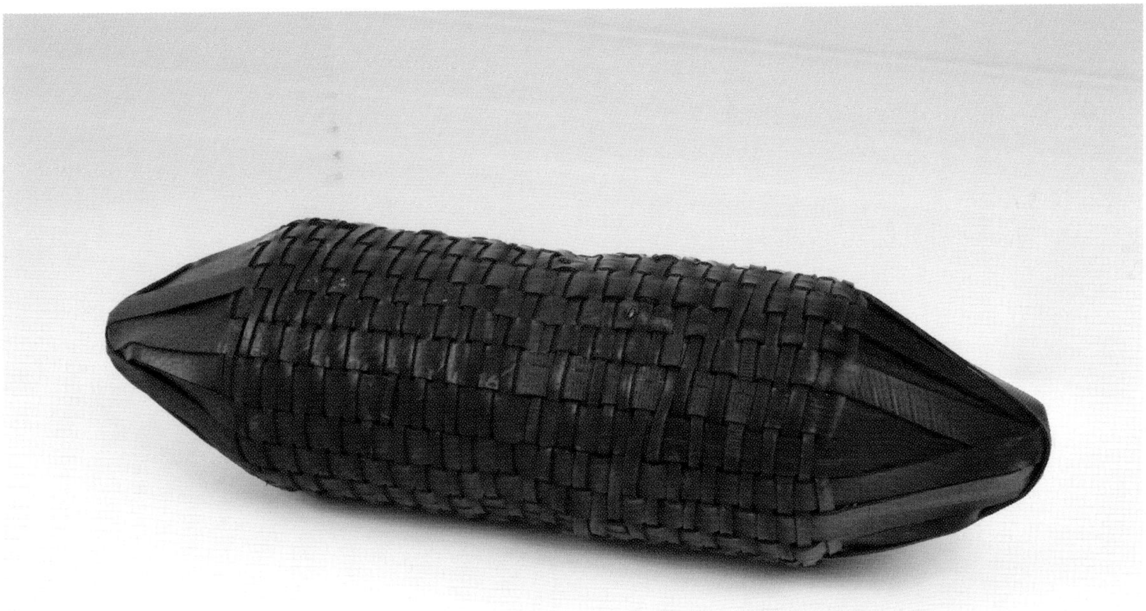

**Knock Out**
1992
rubber over glass
22" x 10" diameter

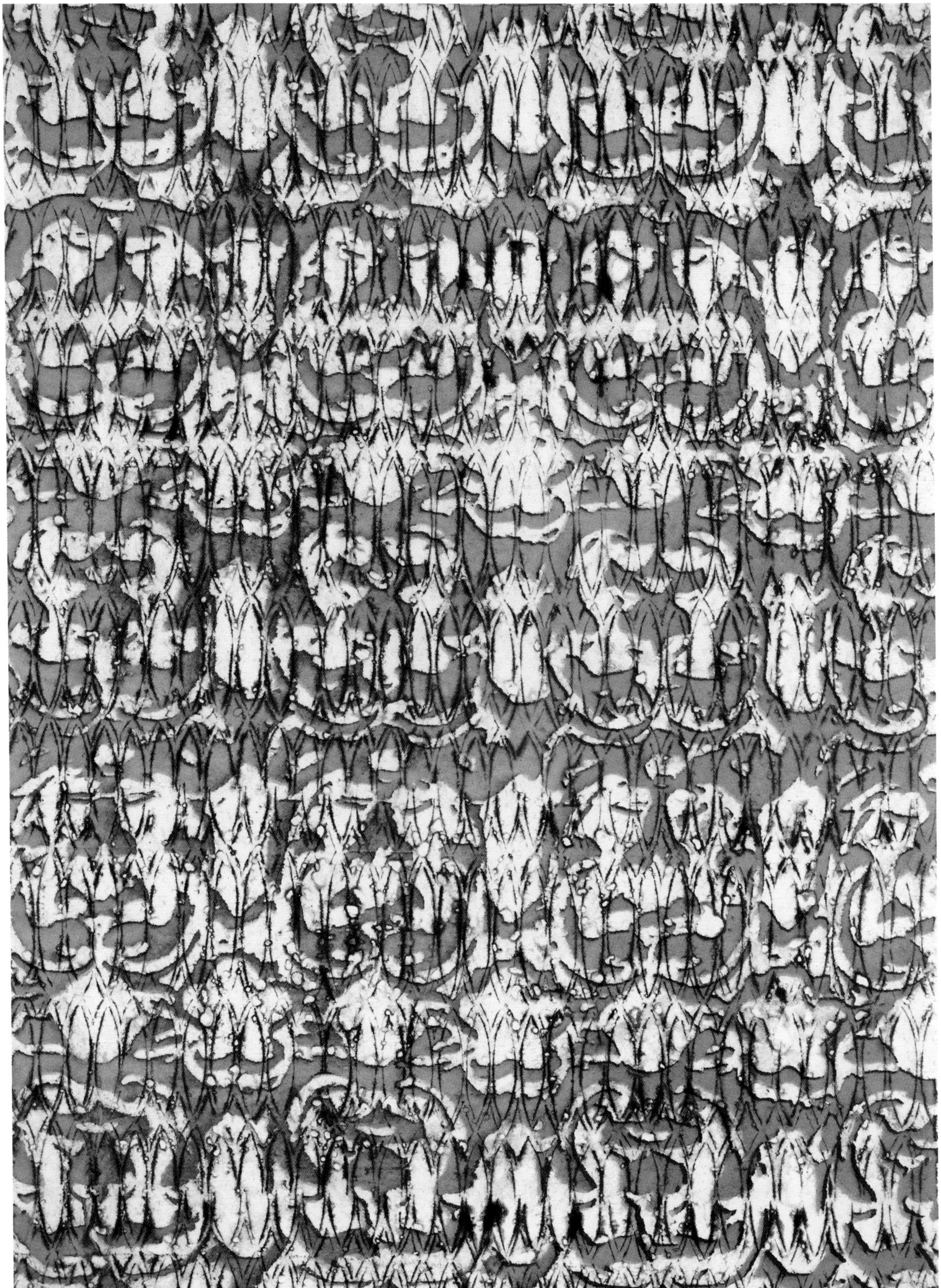

# WAYS TO LEAVE HOME

The celebrated haiku poet Basho went on a writing pilgrimage for 150 days. He walked rain and shine through small towns and mountain passes. On that trip he wrote the book *Oku no Hosomichi*, meaning an Interior, Narrow Road, to evoke both a path to far away places, and his journey of inner reflection. Basho wrote that he did not leave home for this journey but rather that he made his home in the journey. Lanzetta has also traveled to Kyoto, Calcutta, Damascus, Rome, Jakarta, Manila, Bangkok . . . in a similar way. She has not tried to bring back images of the exotic or the stunningly bright. She has endeavored to root herself outside of the places she has known and in that soil tried to grow.

Lanzetta's work exists in a process of constant shifting of place and point of view. There is an ongoing negotiation and construction of how to breathe and live even when the *here* is moving. Steeped in an insistent, physical repetition, Lanzetta makes paintings in a mantra-like practice with infinite variables, subtle shifts and replete motifs. This repetition, like a meditation practice, inscribes into the body, shapes the body and through this cultivates the mind. Her methods suspend assigned meaning and position the work in a process of striving *towards*, rather than setting the work in a fixed destination or place. This can be seen, for example, in the 2007 painting *No Fixed Point*, in which an irregular grid of semi-gloss black circles shadowed with lunar-like pearlescent crescents shifts and shimmers across a field of raised, white enamel lines stamped from industrial auto filters. Lanzetta asks: how do we give up the mooring? How do we uproot? How can we see from a point outside of the place from which we come? How do we see anything beyond a surface view that pins down immediately into an erroneous translation?

In her work, Lanzetta creates a language, not just a spoken language, but an immensely rich and complex cultural palimpsest. This palimpsest encompasses the physical and cultural learning that shapes our personal interactions with one another and how we interpret not just words, but body movements, physical gestures, colors, patterns and proximities. Unsettling the binaries that we normally use to structure meaning, her language creates a multiplicity of new ways to know the world. Within her process, beauty is not in the arrangement but in the in between, after the letting go and before the landing.

Today, we struggle with how to make sense of Basho, how to employ the images of his natural world poetry with our modern, industrial landscape. Lanzetta stunningly negotiates a spiritual practice and inner journey in our contemporary world. She addresses the modern world but is not overwhelmed by it or victim to

*opposite,* **Water Rustle**
1998-99
screenprinted paper
pulp on cotton rag
30" x 22"

it. The industrial, tactile aspects of these paintings show a willingness to see the world around us, not in an idealized way, but through the materials of its construction: gritty, rough, oversized and chemical. Through these materials of the natural and industrial, Lanzetta paints how we forage a human life with conflict, points of beauty and emotional, spiritual connections. These connections are of an artist to the world around her but also have a space open for us to step into this process of making, and through it to connect to the world and each other.

*Judy Halebsky*
*Tokyo, May 2010*

*Judy Halebsky is a poet who divides her time between Tokyo and San Francisco. She is an editor and translator for the bilingual poetry journal,* Eki Mae. *Her book,* Sky=Empty, *won the 2009 New Issues Poetry Prize.*

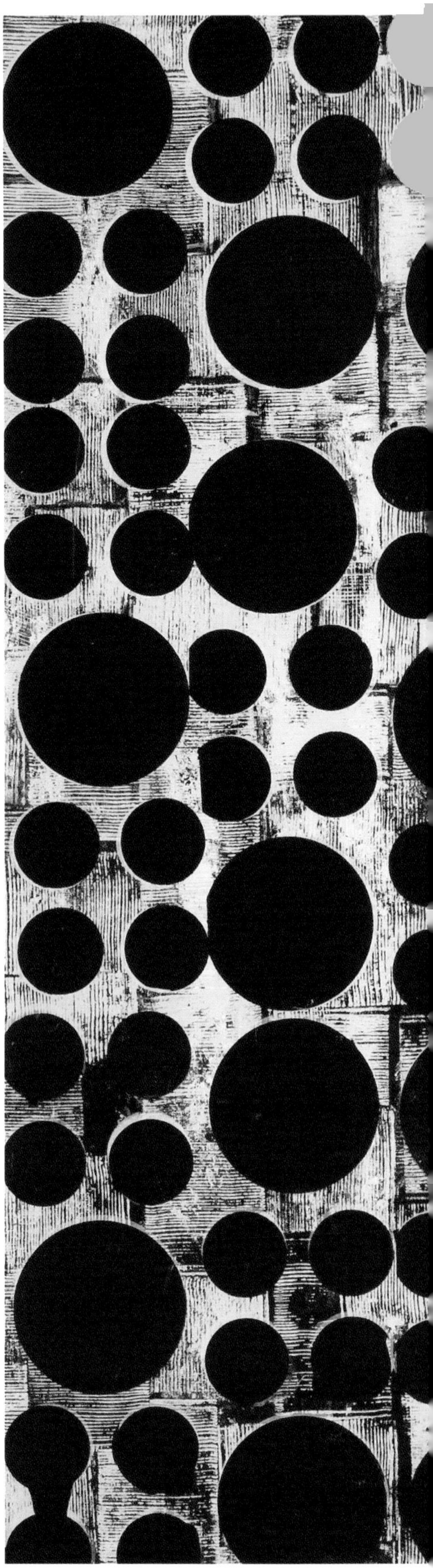

**No Fixed Point**
2007-8
oil, enamel, and acrylic on canvas
52" x 60"

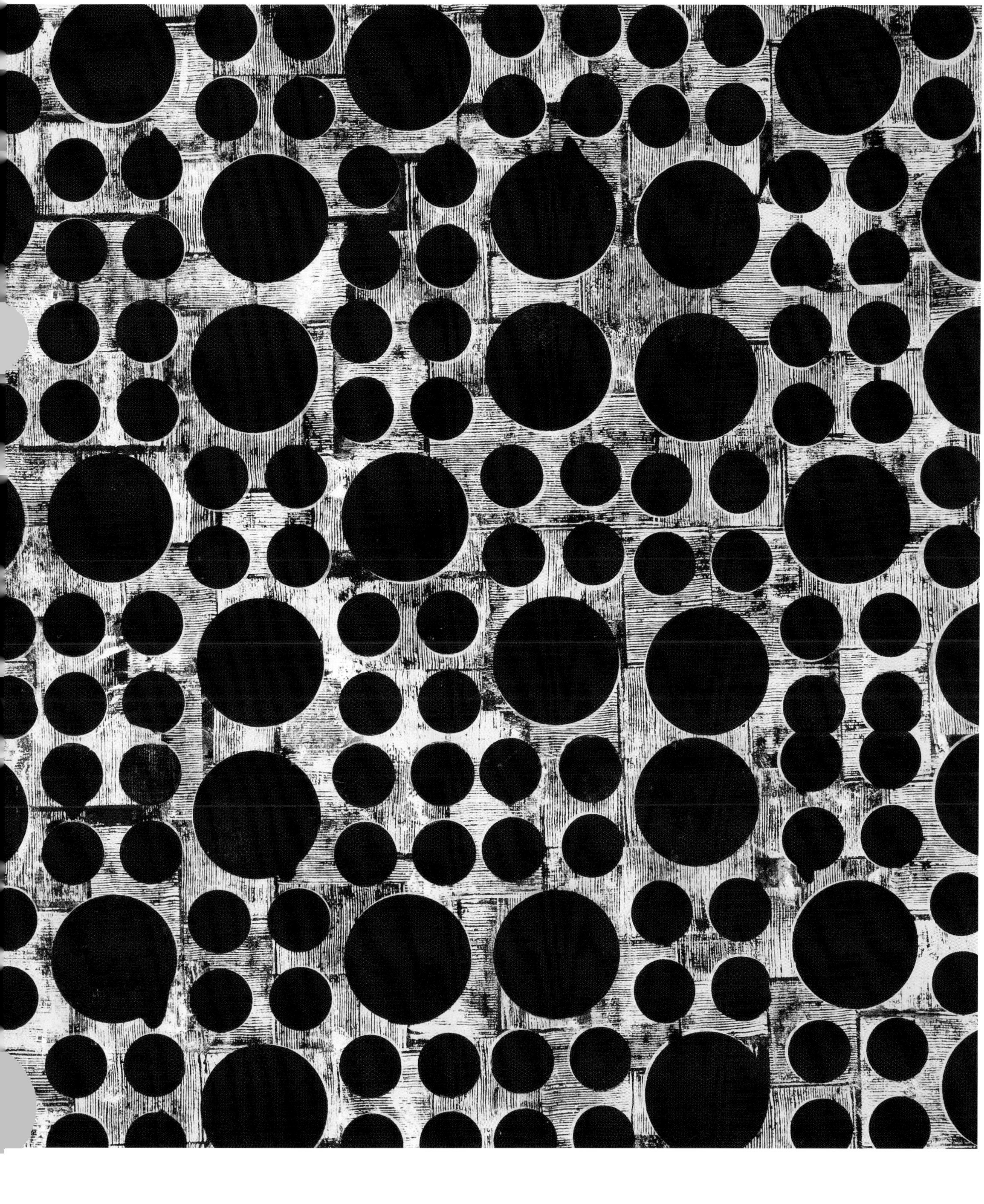

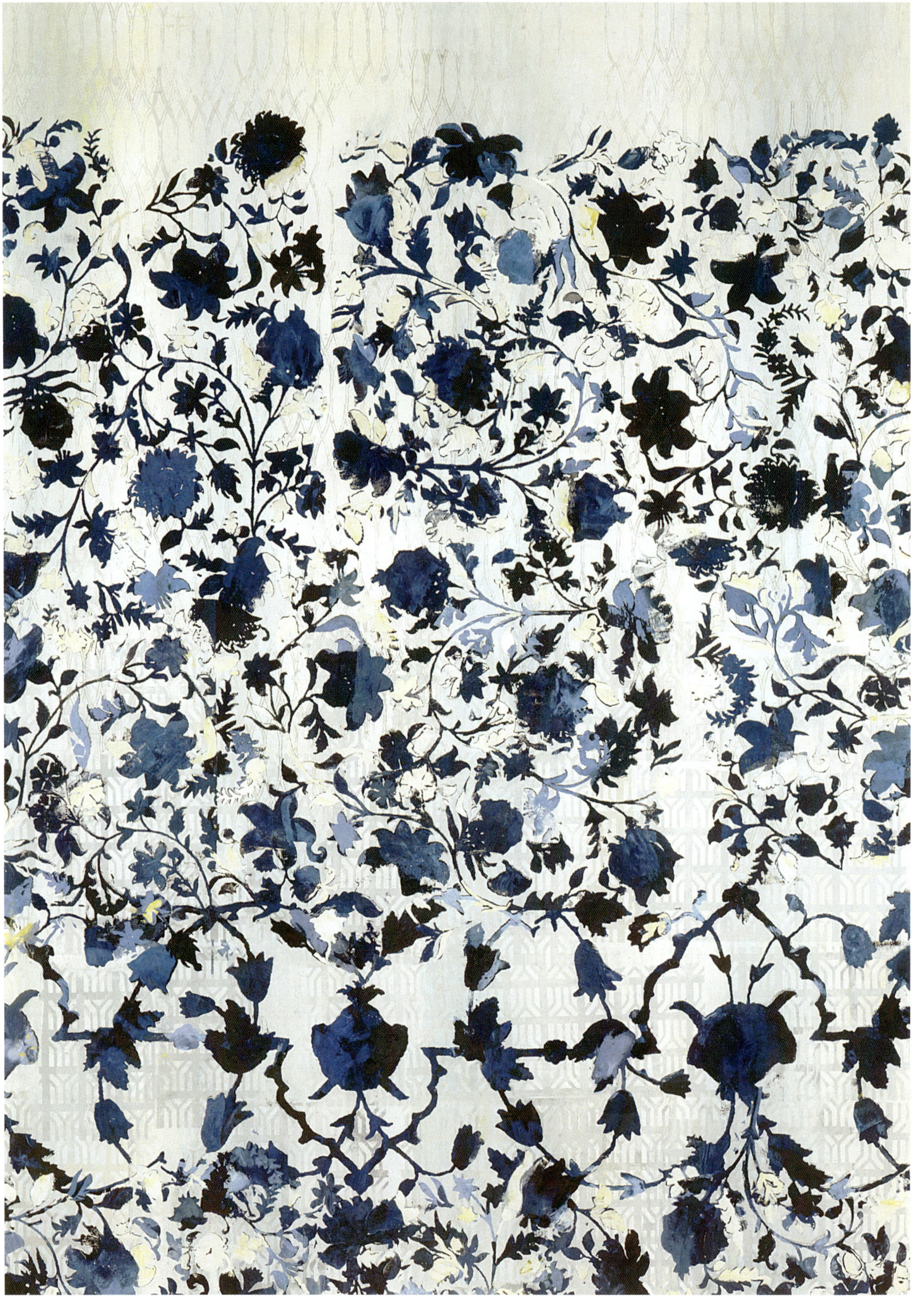

# CHRONOLOGY OF WORKS BY SERIES

**Never Let Me Go 1990-1992**
Arcanta Group
Bandgare
Knock Out
Korb
Long Sack/Collar
Popotoafd
Short Sack/Collar
Torso

**A Bangkok Love Map (one breadth at a Time) 1992**
Untitled (head)
Untitled (torso)

**Evidence from the Vernacular 1996-1997**
Black Snow
Delivery
Field
Syncopation
Permutation II
U.T. (Breath)
U.T. (Call to Prayer)
U.T. (Double Mass Shawl)
U.T. (Songket)
U.T. (Sumatra)
U.T. (Wings)

**Brittle Spring 1998-1999**
Black Bead Game
Glass Bead Game
Night Map
Strangeness of Beauty
Water Rustle

**Blow Space 1991-2000**
Blow Space
Broken Serenade
Dreamless
Midnight Syntax
Science Punk
Swoon Song
Tracery

**Cultural Instructions 2001-04**
Air Map
Ambidextrous
Cultural Instruction I
Eternity In An Hour
Flirt
Juvenilia
Lust Card
Nightshade
Philanderer
Sonatina
Taxonomy
Wild Card
Winsome Friend

**Recitativo Series 2002-2005**
Glassblower II
Midsummer's Marriage I (Tippett)
Midsummer's Marriage II (Tippett)

**The Confection Series* 2005-2006**
Distant Theatres
Lilypad Deployment I
Lotus(cayenne)
Relic Species
Tattoo (green)
Tattoo (magenta)
Tattoo (red)

**Echolalia, The Forgetting of Language 2007**
Echolalia, The Forgetting of Language N. 2
Echolalia, The Forgetting of Language N. 3
Echolalia, The Forgetting of Language N. 4
Echolalia, The Forgetting of Language N. 15

**Black Diamond Express 2008-2009**
BDE 2
BDE 7
BDE 11
BDE 13

**game*Space* 2007-2010**
Across the Black Water
Biophilia: Eve
Empire
It's All Spiritual
Last Two Million
No Fixed Point
Signal Jumping, Black
Stylish Show-Up
The Same Winter

**Company Paintings 2009**
Ballary 0839
Beed 0244
Belur 0832
Howrah 0322
Indore 0731
Jorhat 0376
Karnal 0184
Musiri 0432

**American Time 2010**
Diamondville
Ten Sleep
Transfer Effect
White Sulphur

All works courtesy of the artist unless otherwise noted.
* from information designer Edward Tufte's "confections": hybrids of different data, annealed and cooked into a single shallow plane

*opposite,*
**Taxonomy**
2001
oil, enamel, and acrylic on canvas 56" x 40"
Collection of Barbara Kelly, Canada

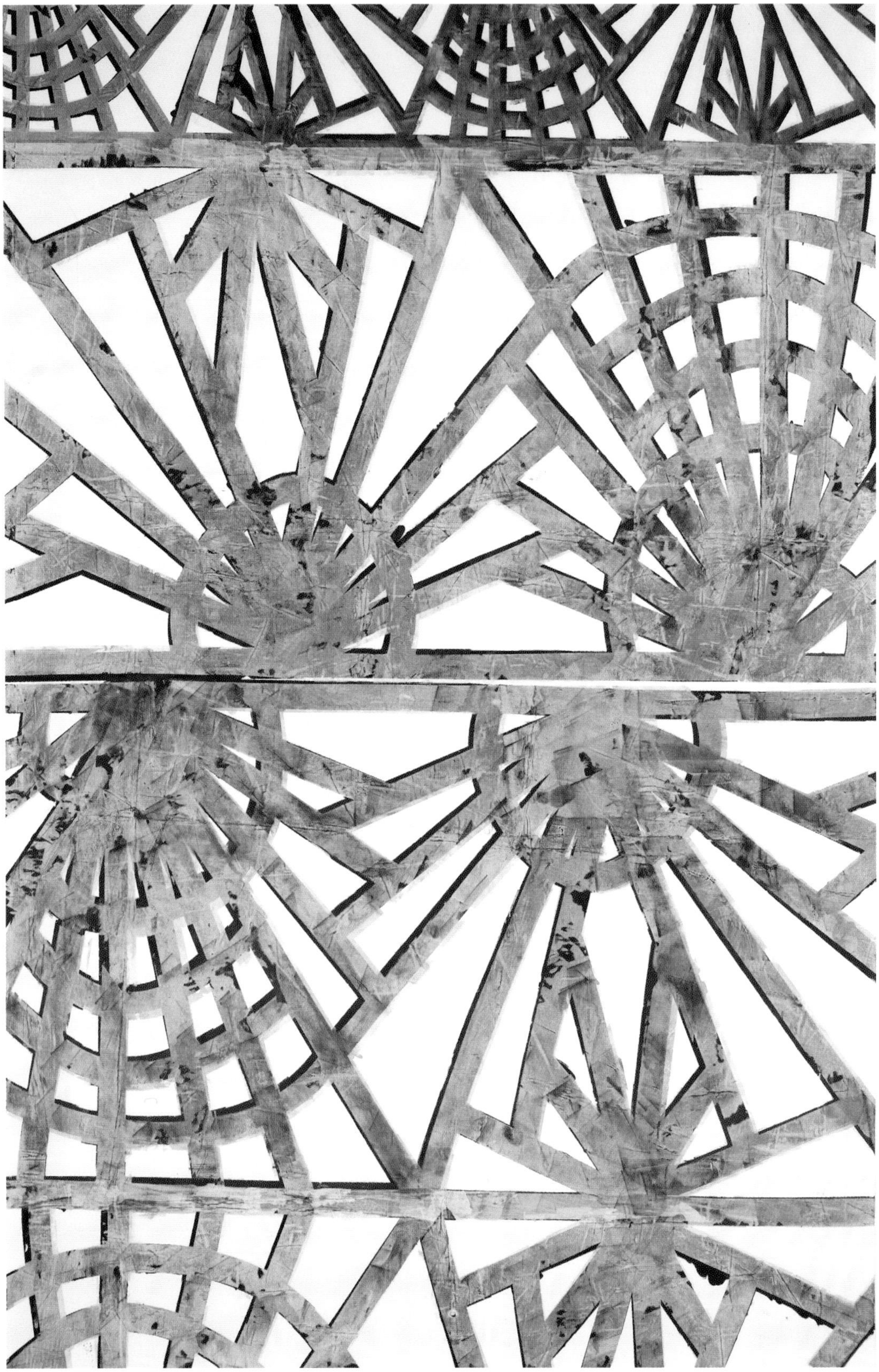

**Ten Sleep**
2010
acrylic on paper
40" x 26"

*opposite,*
**Korb**
1990
rubber, wood, graphite and steel
50" x 28" diameter

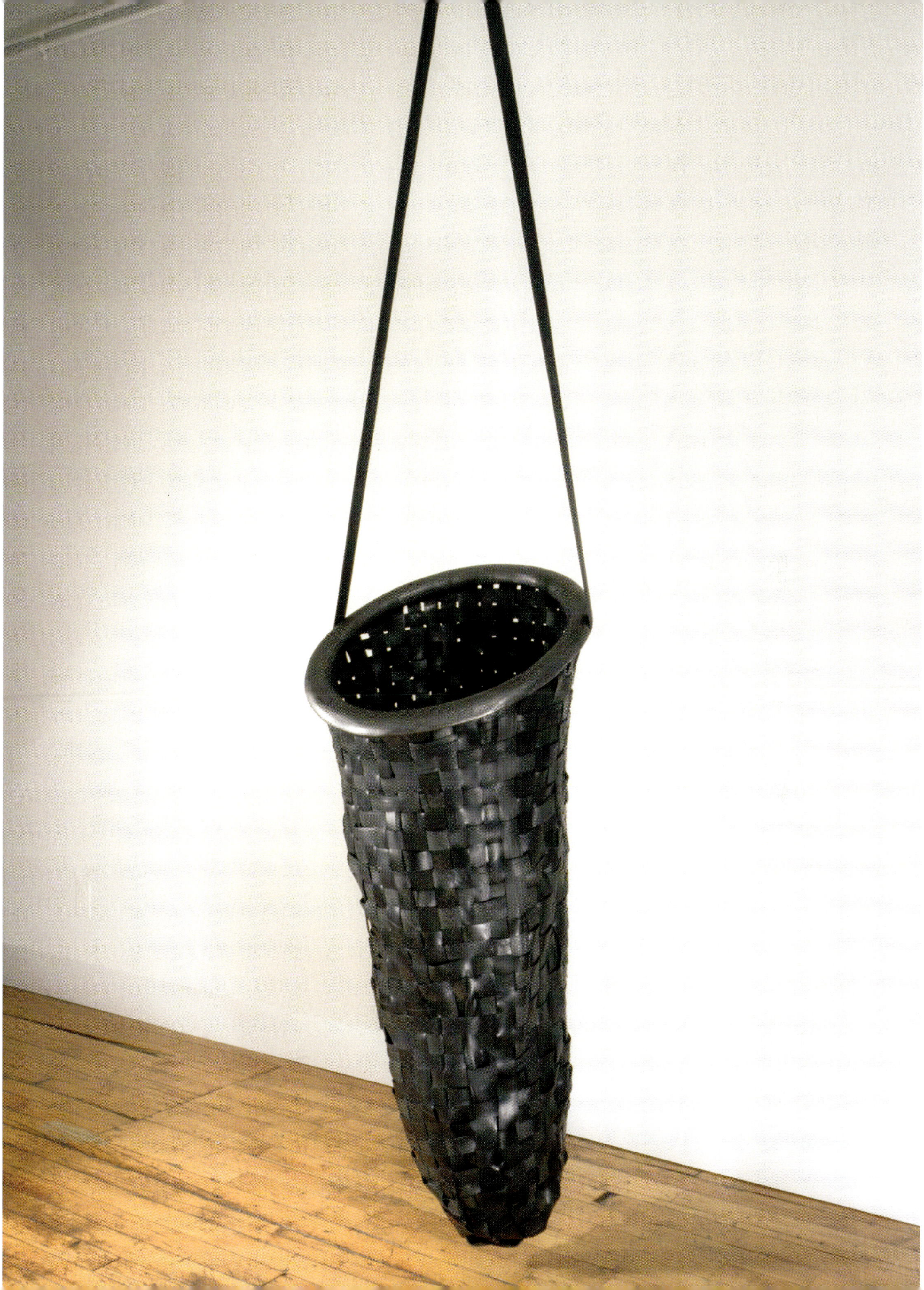

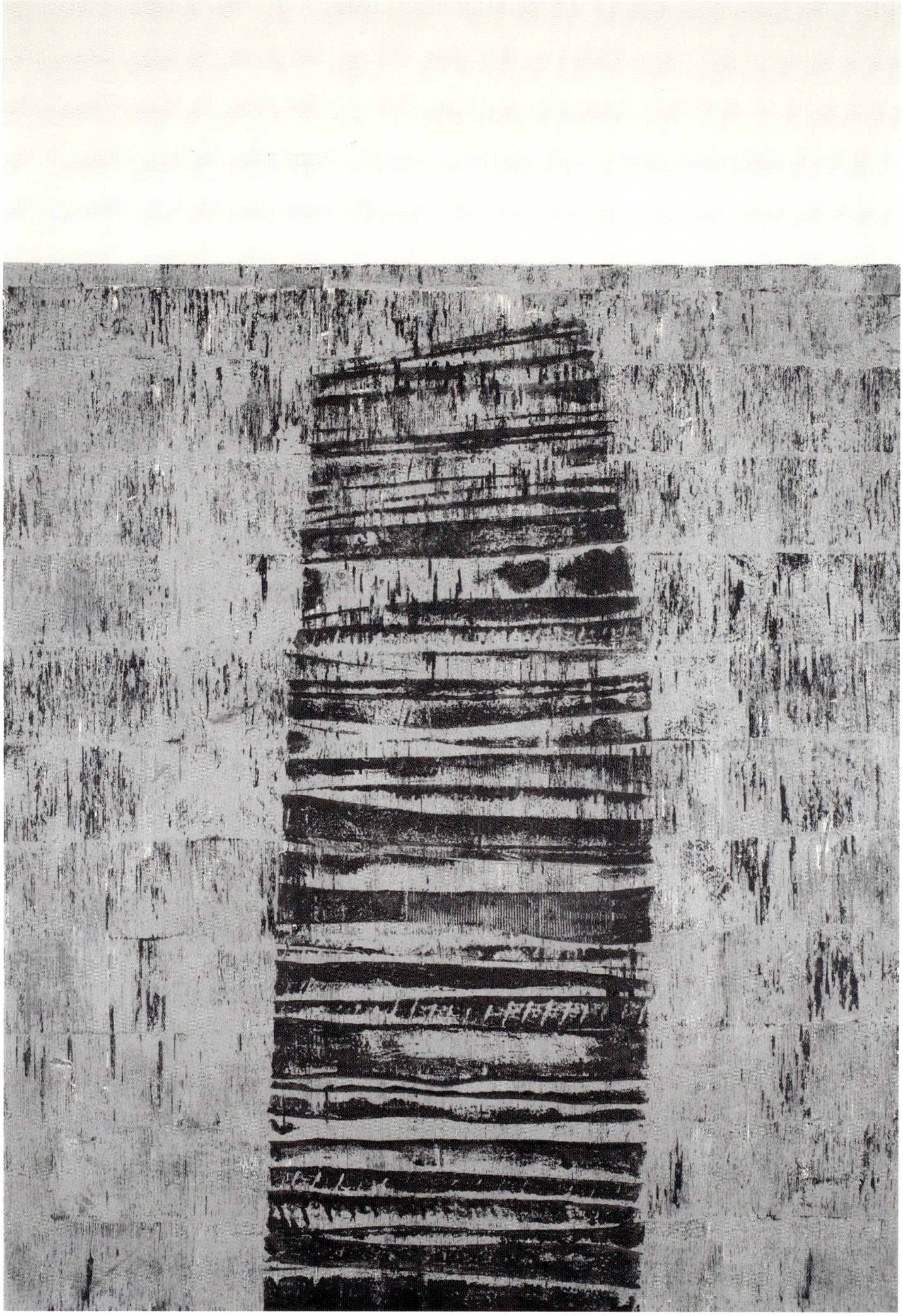

**Untitled (torso)**
1992
ink on paper
40" x 28"

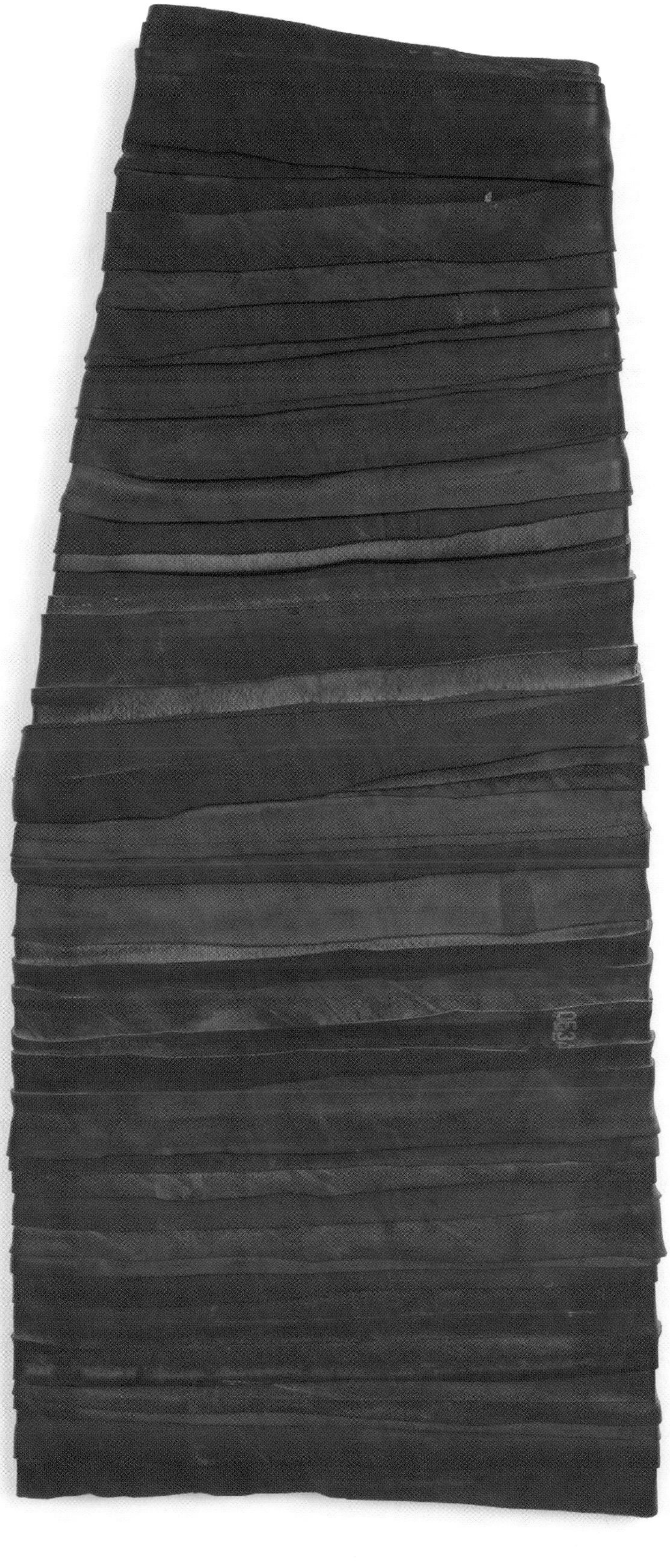

**Torso**
1990
rubber and wood
24" x 11" x 2"

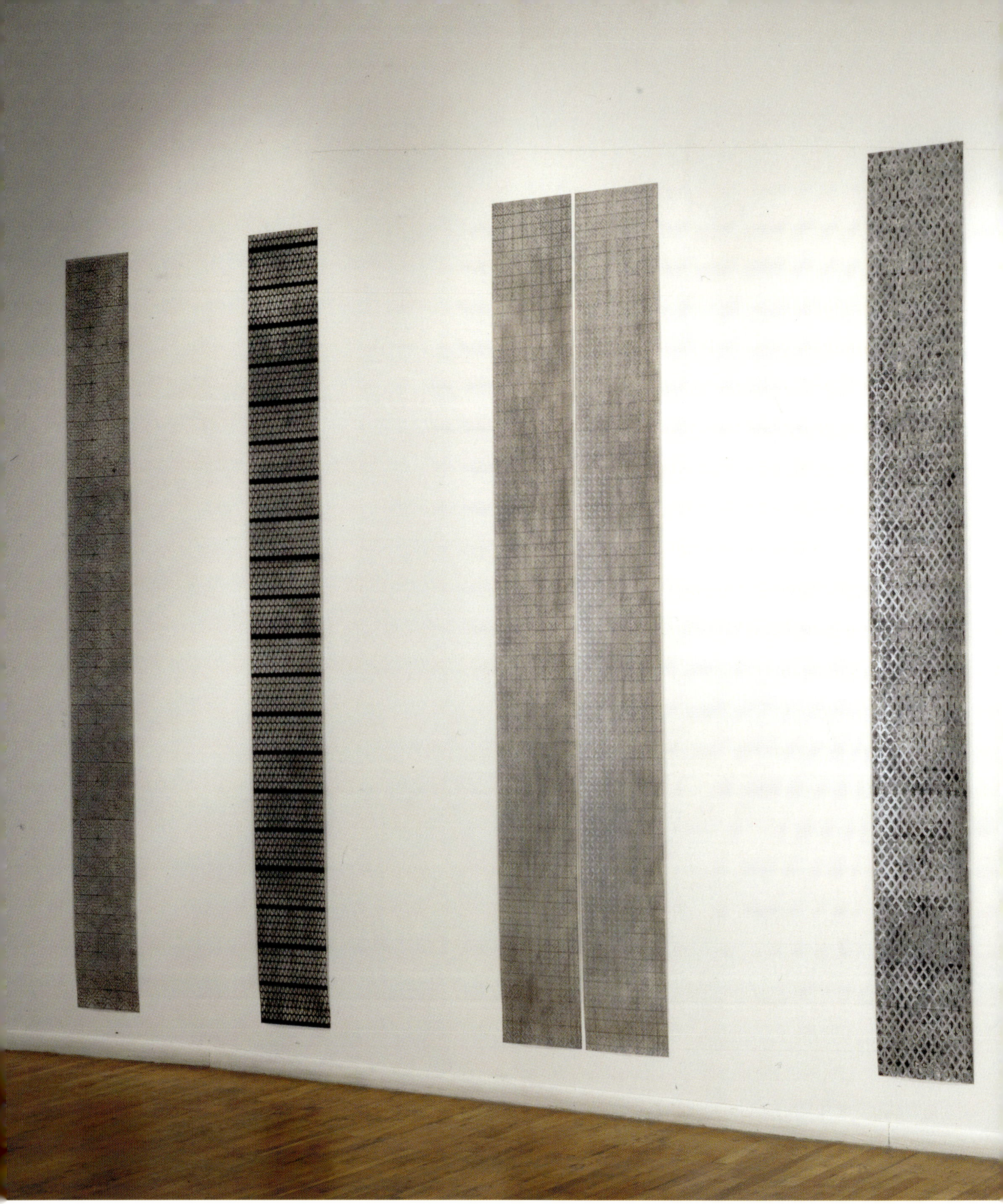

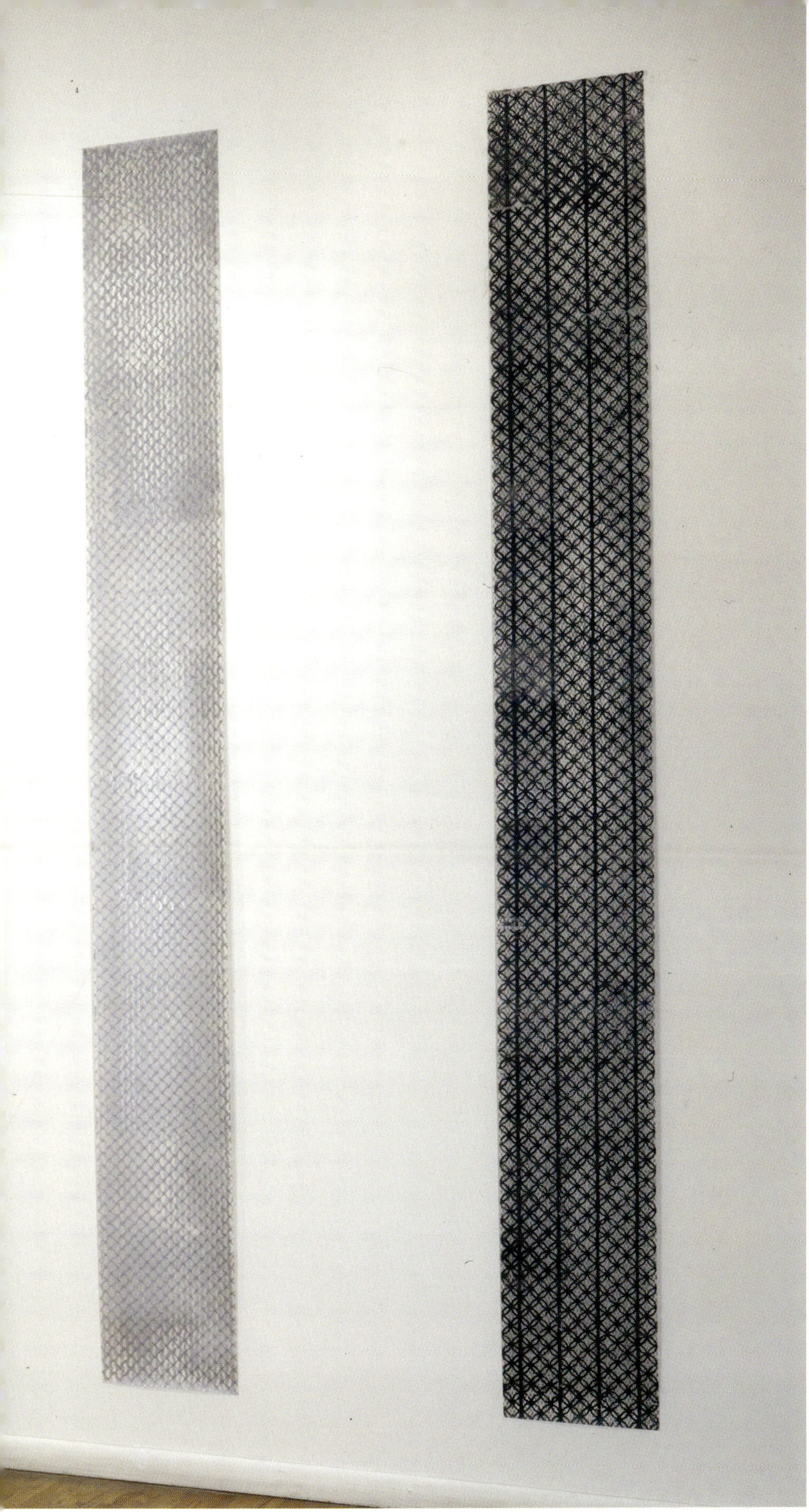

***New Work*** Kim Foster Gallery, New York.
solo exhibition 1997
*(from left to right):* **Untitled (Call to Prayer)**, 1996,
**Permutation II**, 1996, **Double Mass Shawl**, 1996,
**Untitled (Songket)**, 1996, **Untitled (Breath)**, 1997,
**Untitled (Sumatra)**, 1997
each painting: acrylic, enamel, and polyurethane
on mylar, 120" x 14"

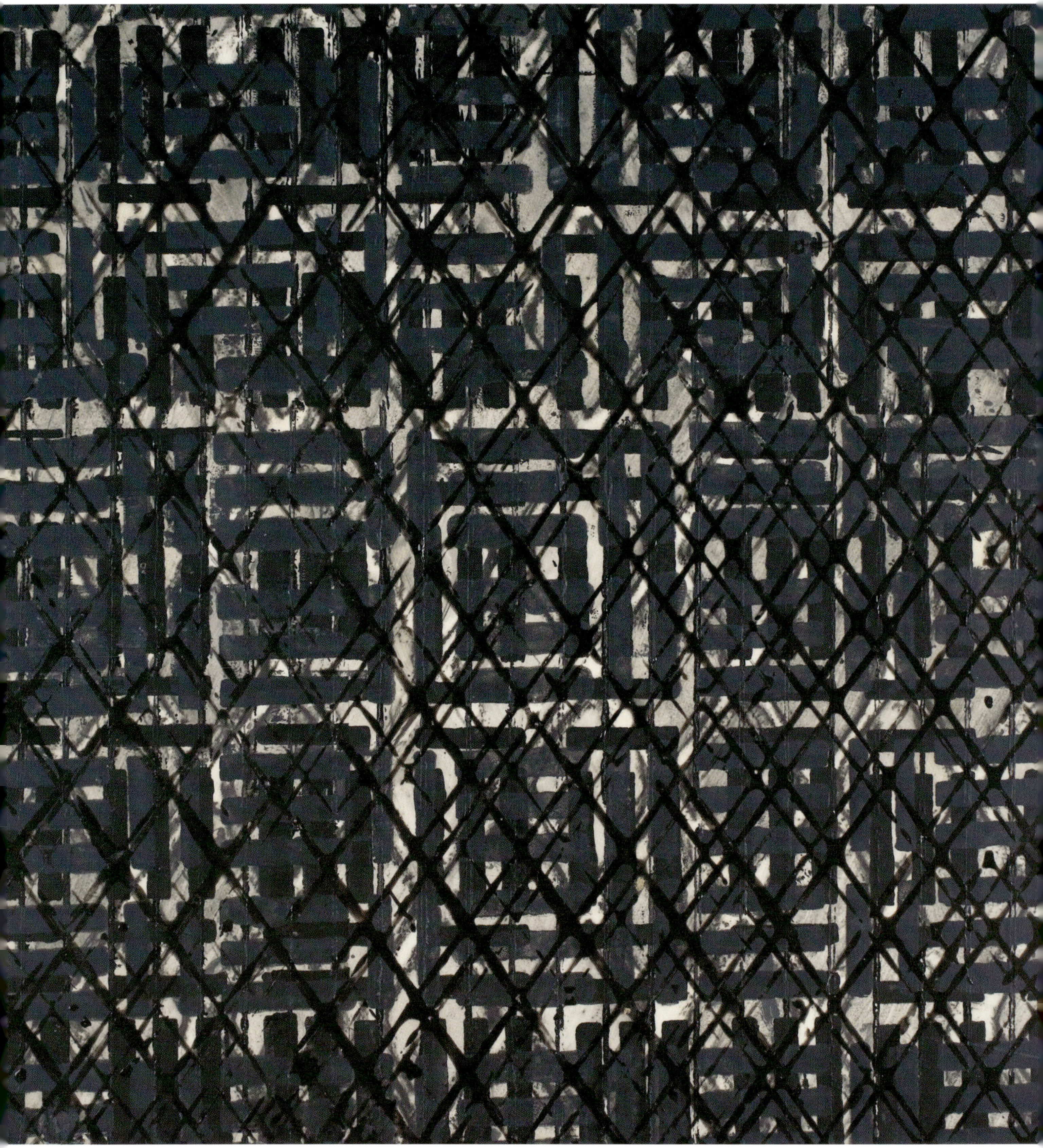

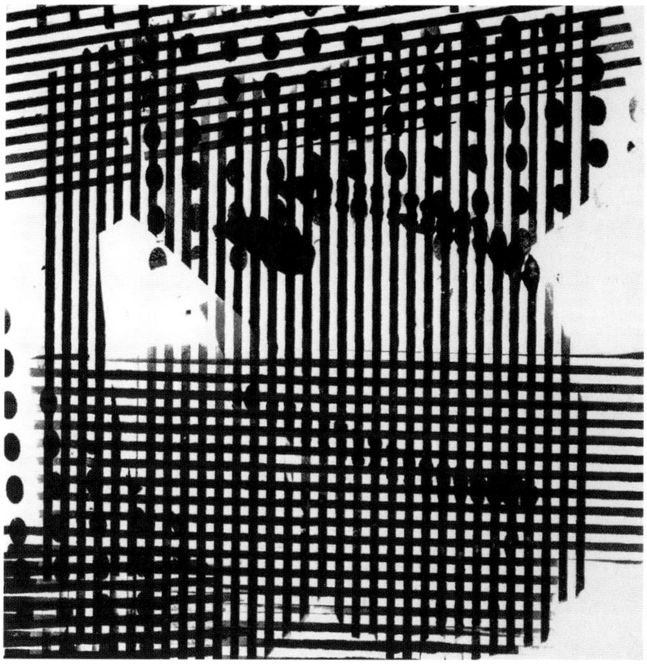

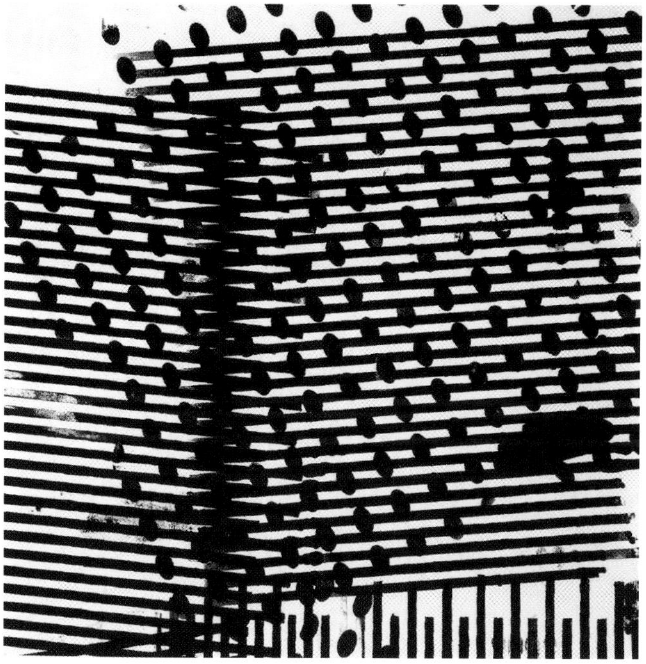

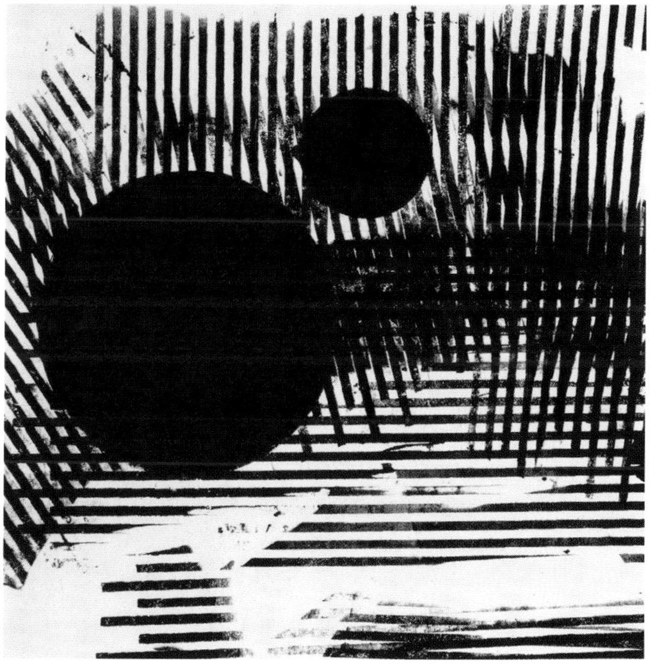

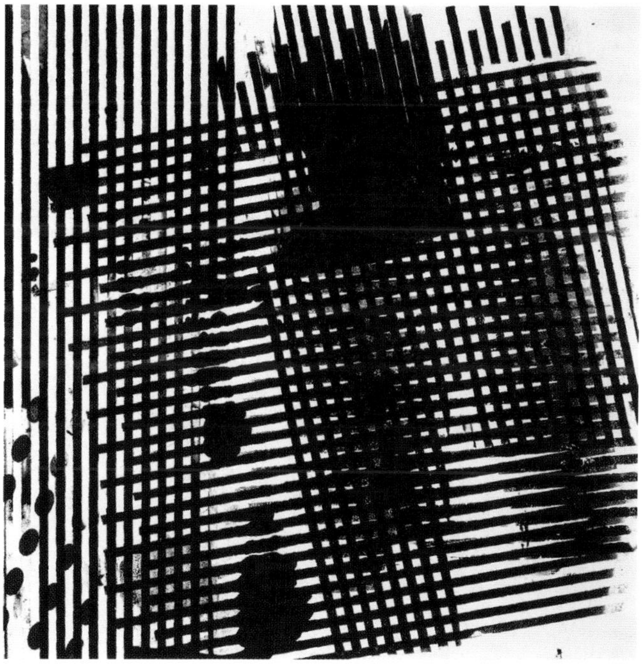

*top left,*
**BDE 7**
2009
acrylic on handmade
Indian paper
15" x 15"

*bottom left,*
**BDE 2**
2009
acrylic on handmade
Indian paper
15" x 15"

*top right,*
**BDE 13**
2009
acrylic on handmade
Indian paper
15" x 15"

*bottom right,*
**BDE 11**
2009
acrylic on handmade
Indian paper
15" x 15"

*opposite,*
**Midnight Syntax**
1999
acrylic on mylar on panel
14" x 14"
Collection of Niall Worn,
Germany

**Field**
1995
enamel on mylar
120" x 42"

*opposite,*
**Stylish Show-Up**
2010
oil, enamel, and acrylic on canvas
60" x 52"

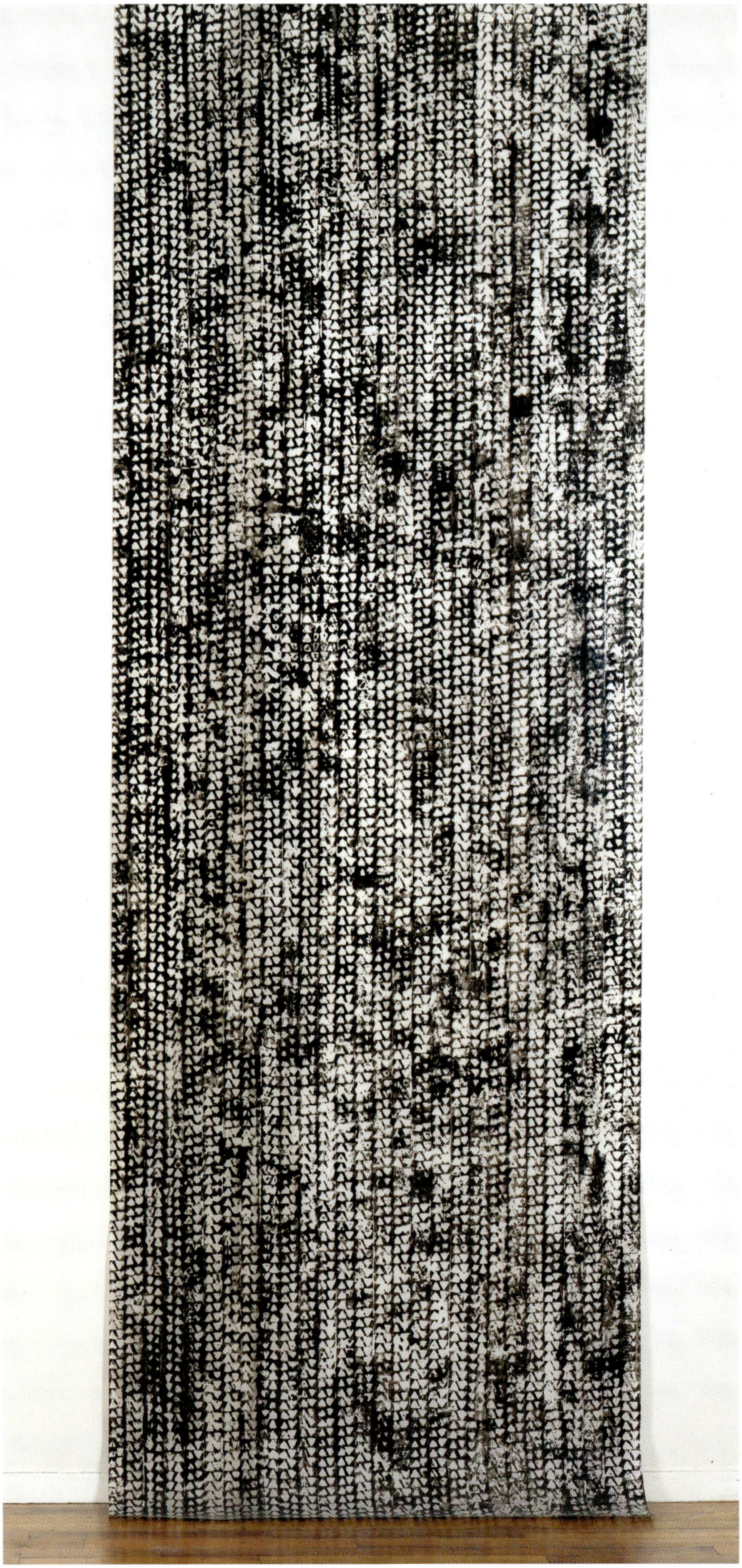

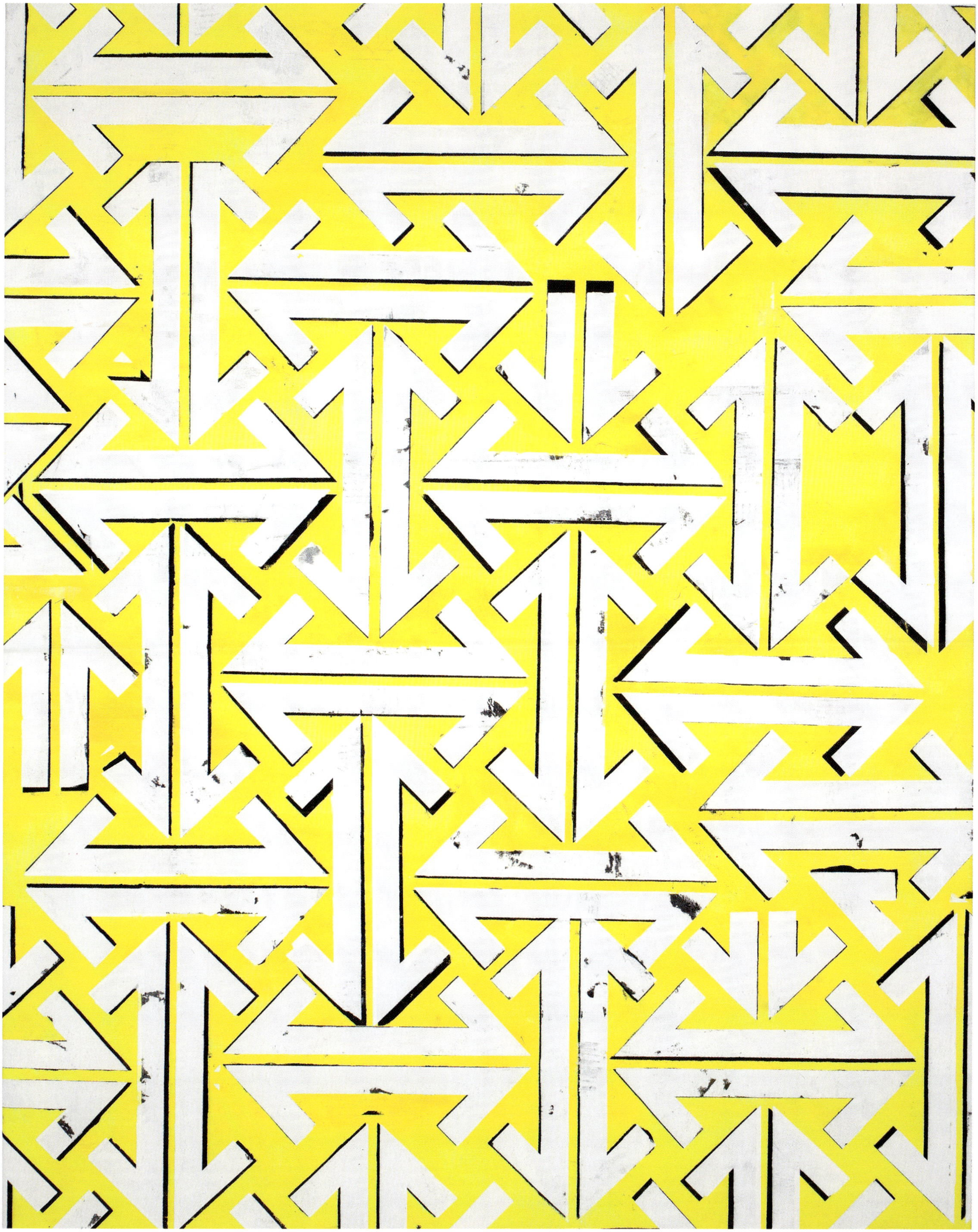

**Relic Species**
2006
enamel, acrylic, and mixed
media on canvas mounted
on panel
36" x 50"

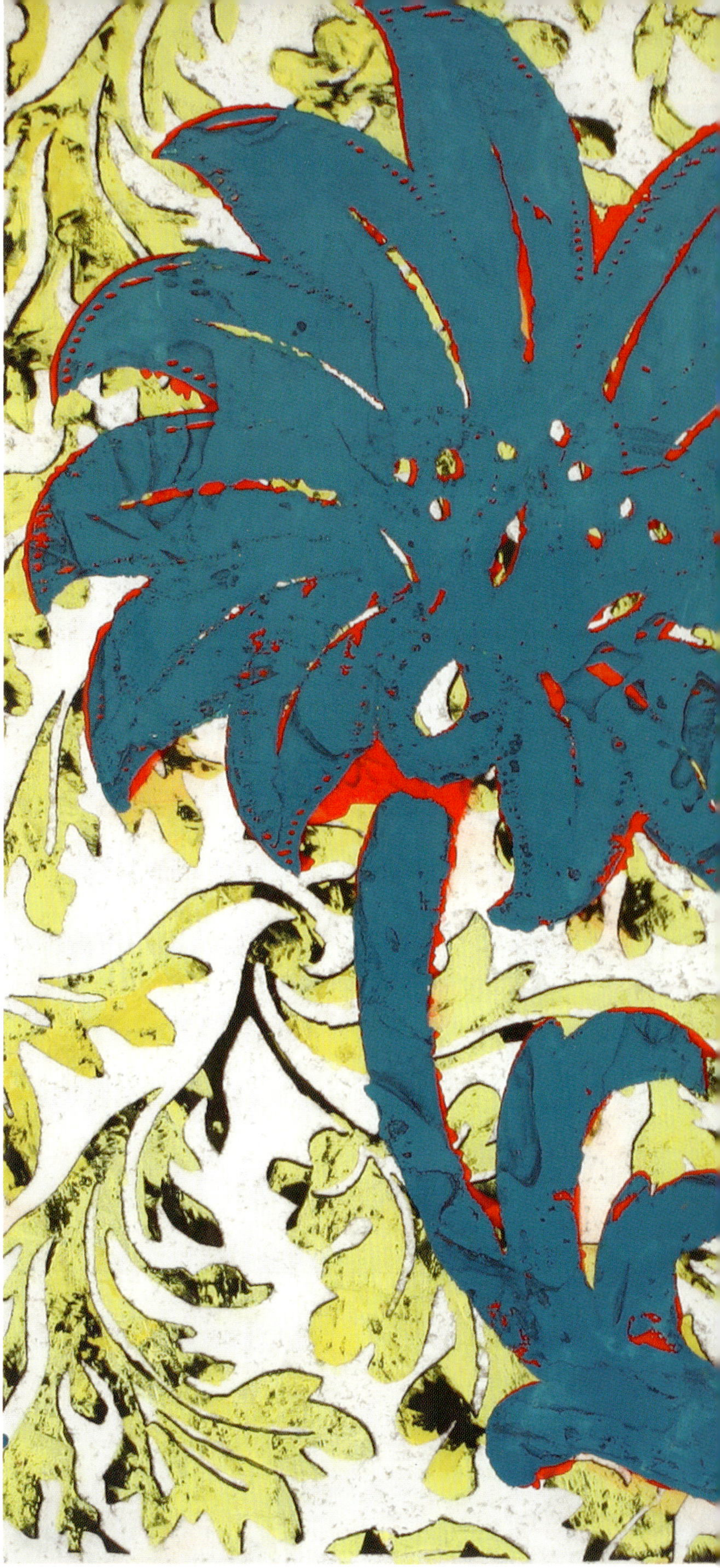

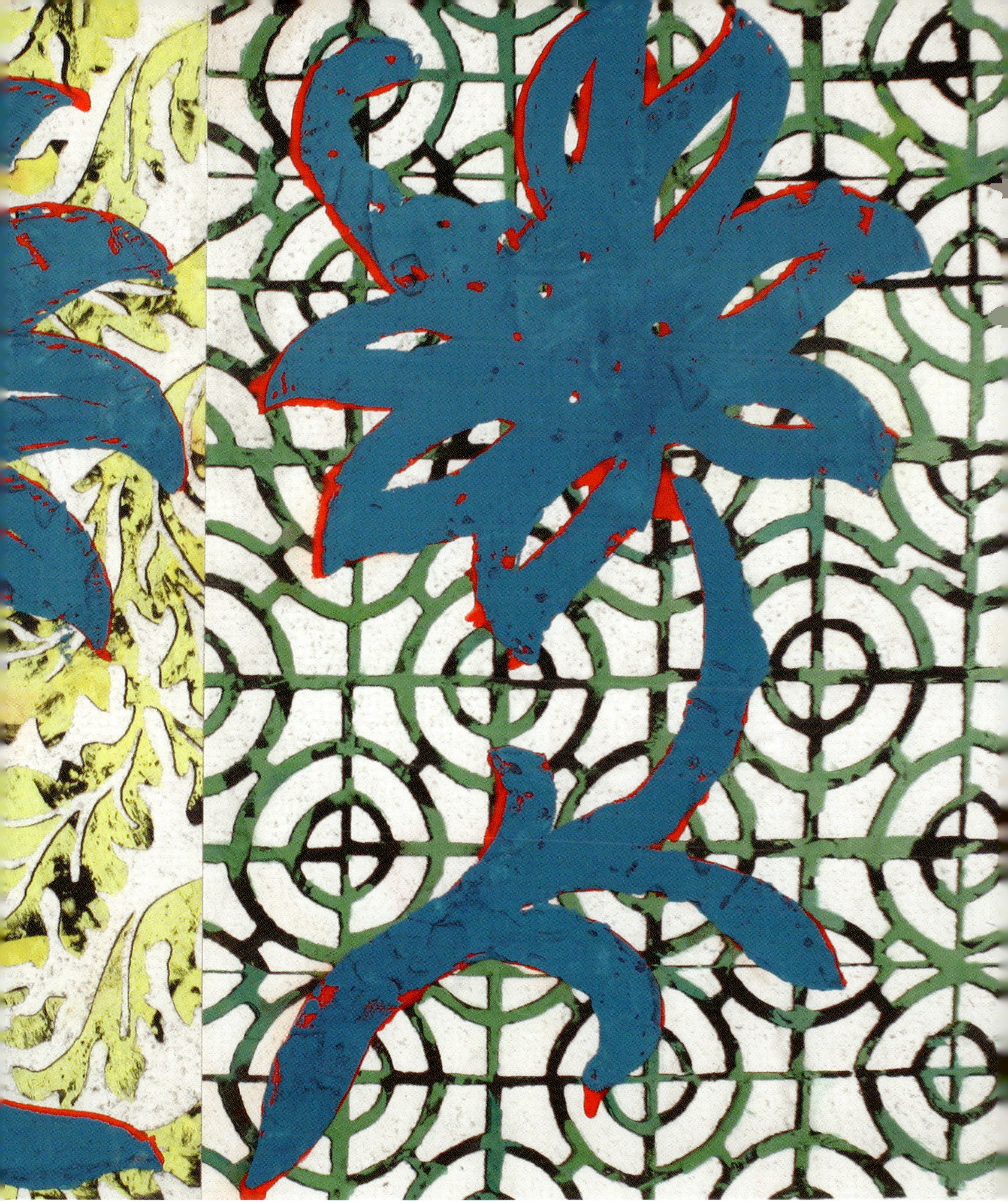

**Karnal 0184**
2010
oil and enamel on panel
24" x 24"

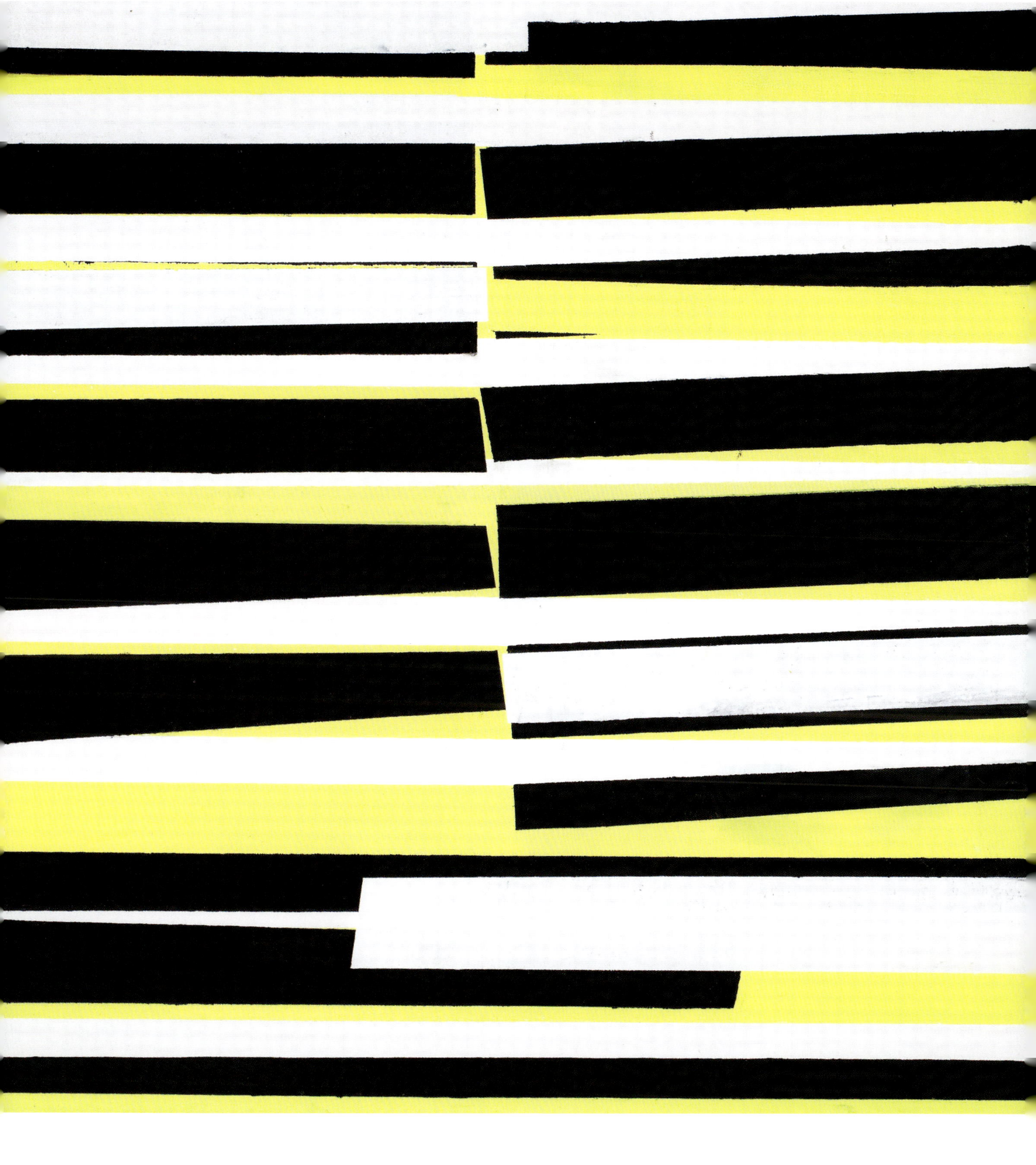

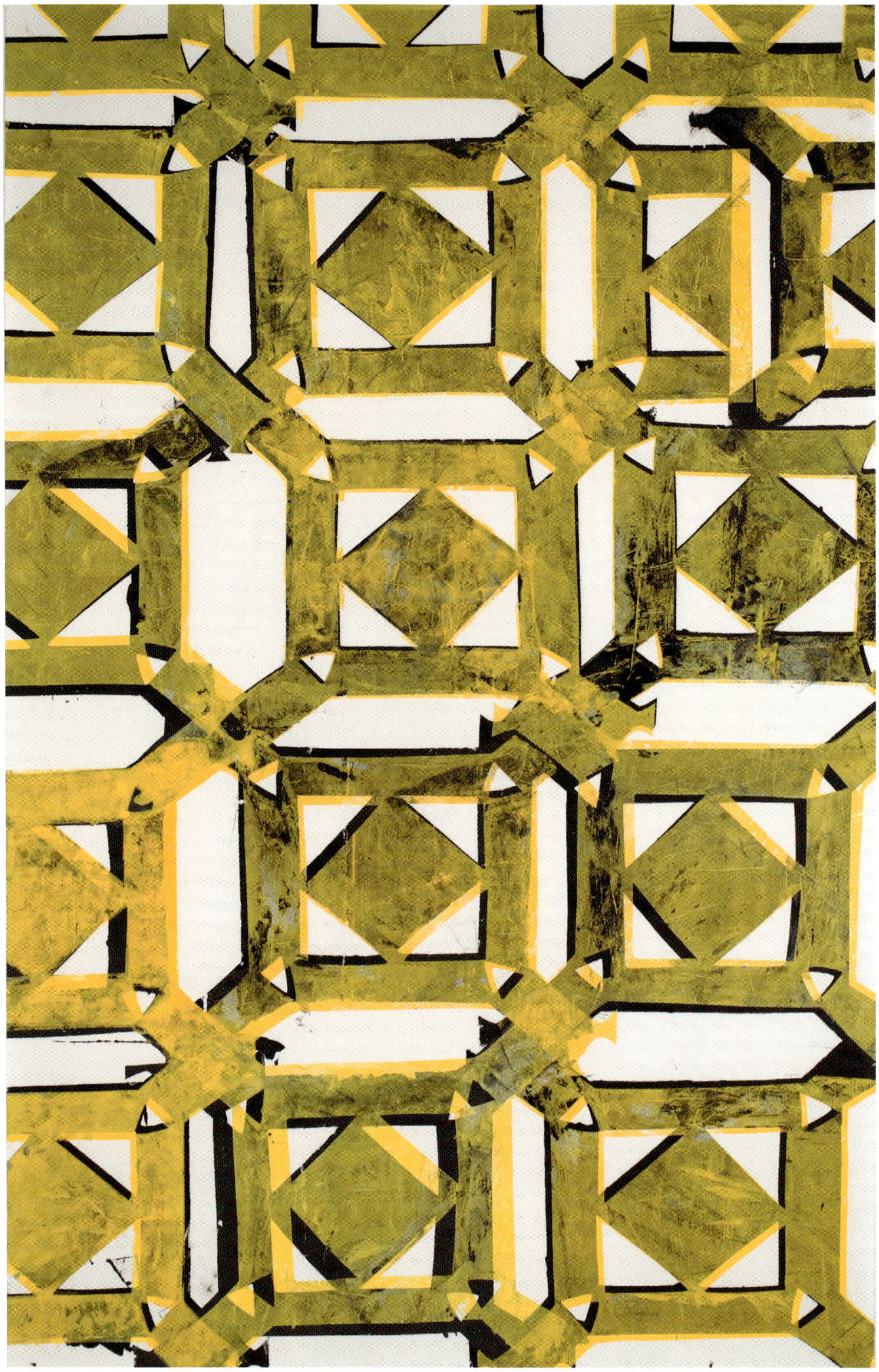

**Diamondville**
2010
acrylic on paper
40" x 26"

**Air Map**
2004
oil, enamel, and acrylic
on canvas
56" x 40 "

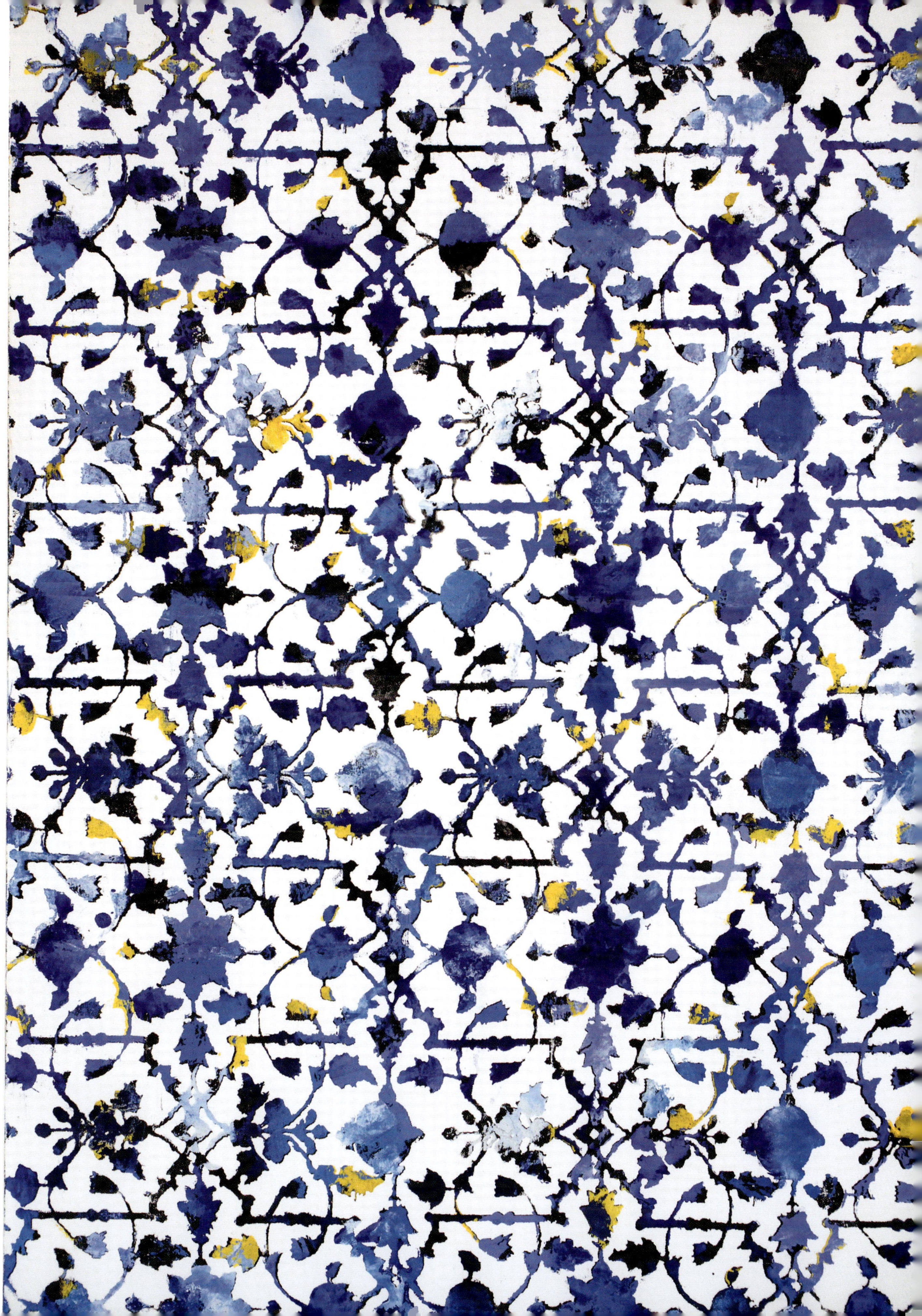

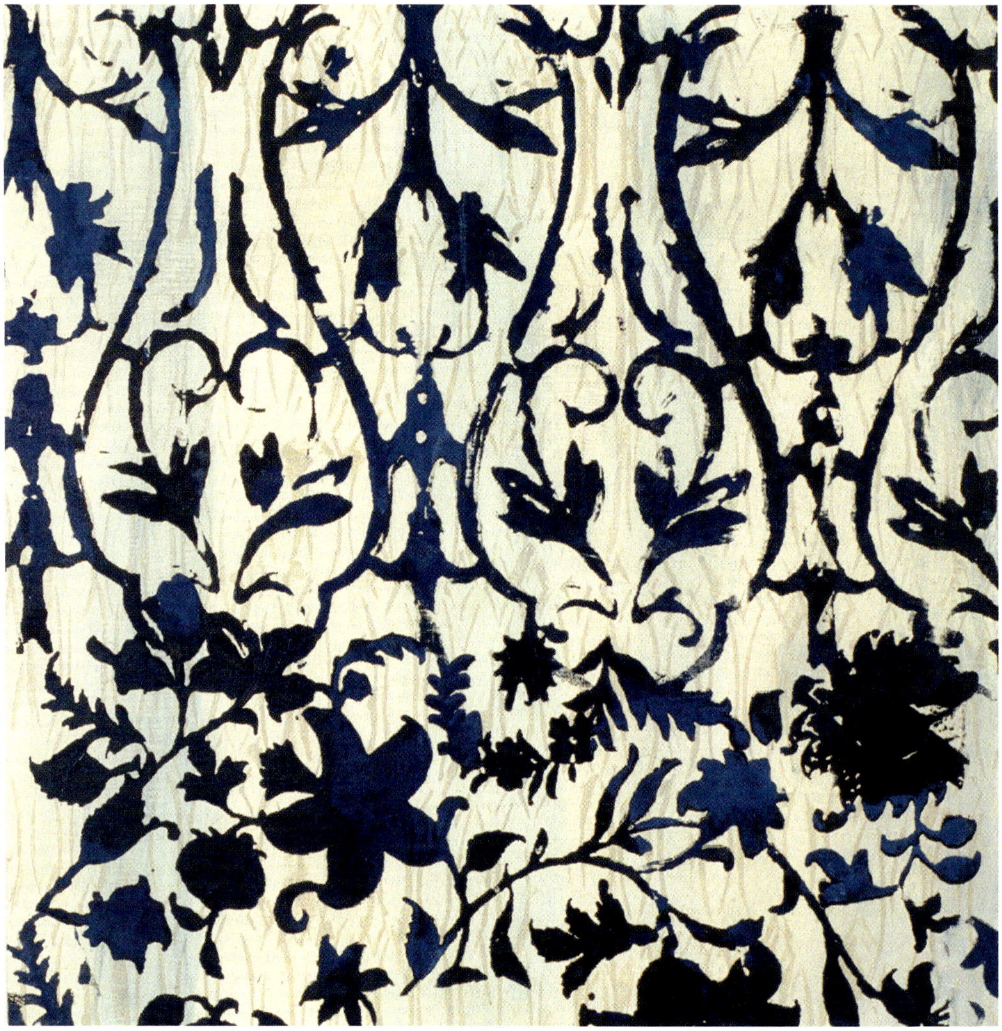

**Sonatina**
2001
oil, enamel, and acrylic on panel
17" x 17"
Collection of Natasha and Ross Taylor, Australia

**Philanderer**
2001
oil and enamel on panel
36" x 27"
Collection of the Victoria and Albert Museum. Purchased through the Julie and Robert Breckman Print Fund

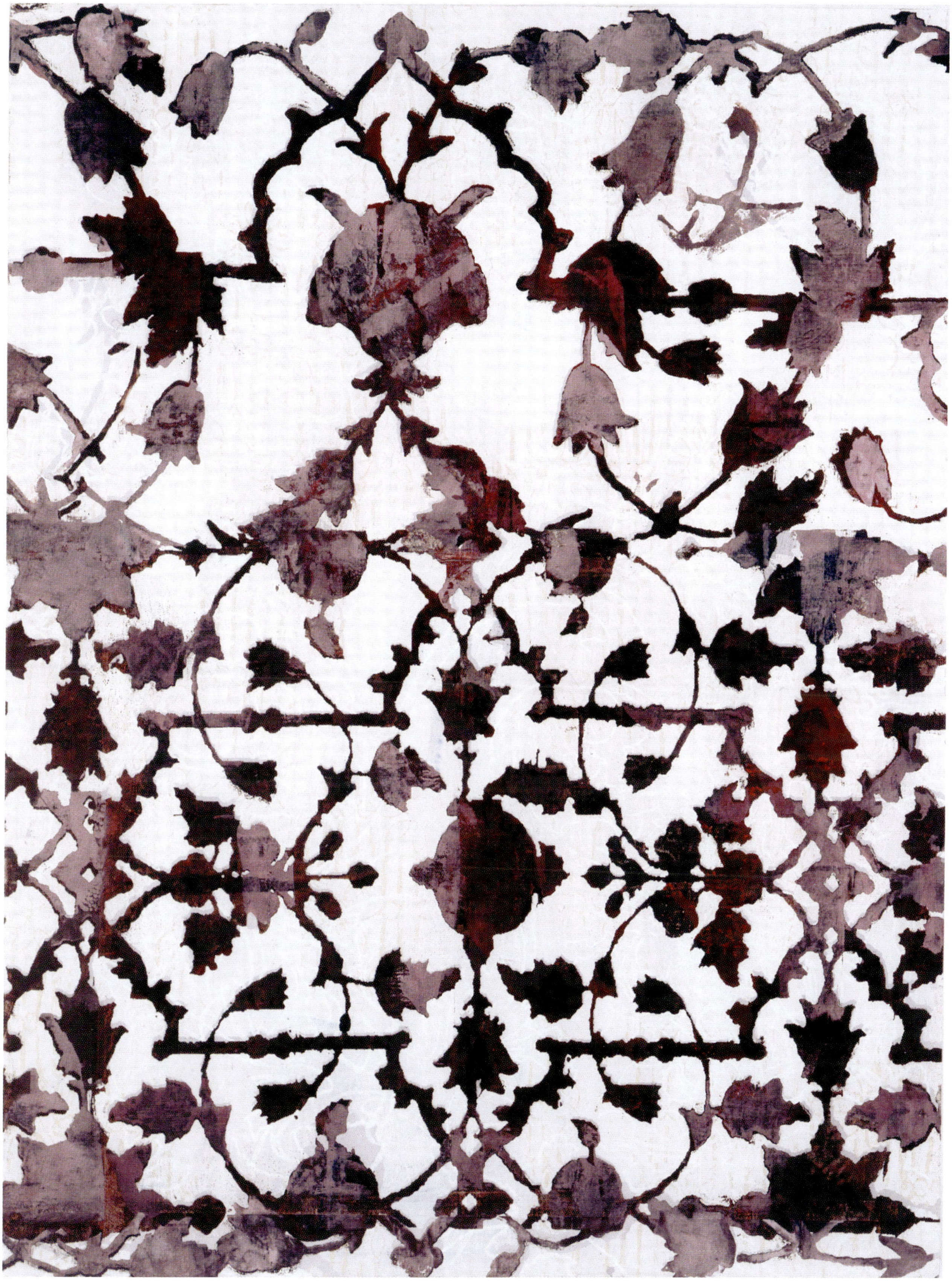

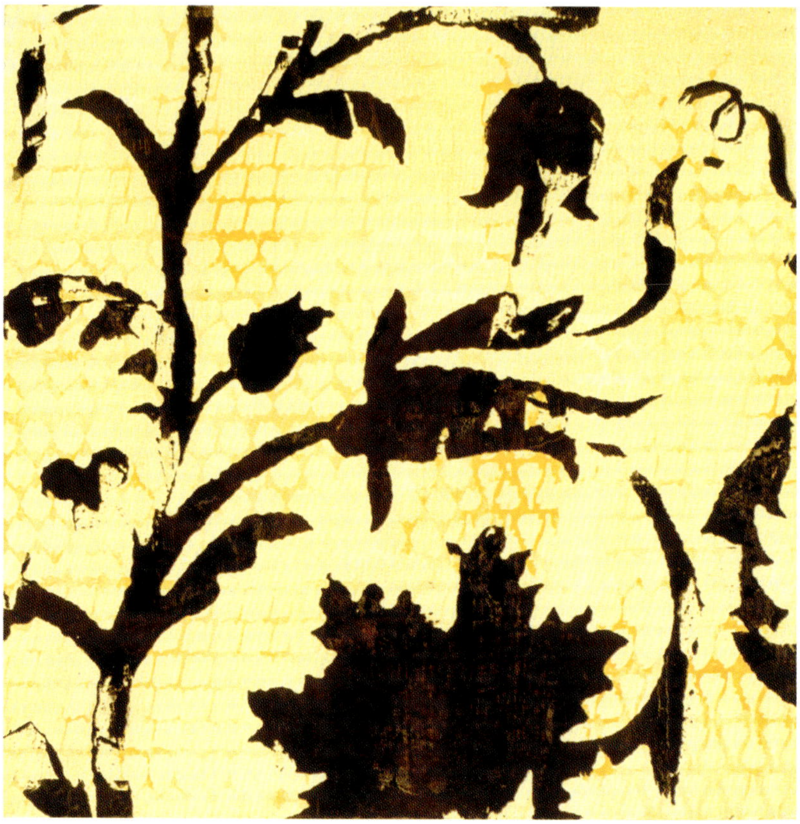

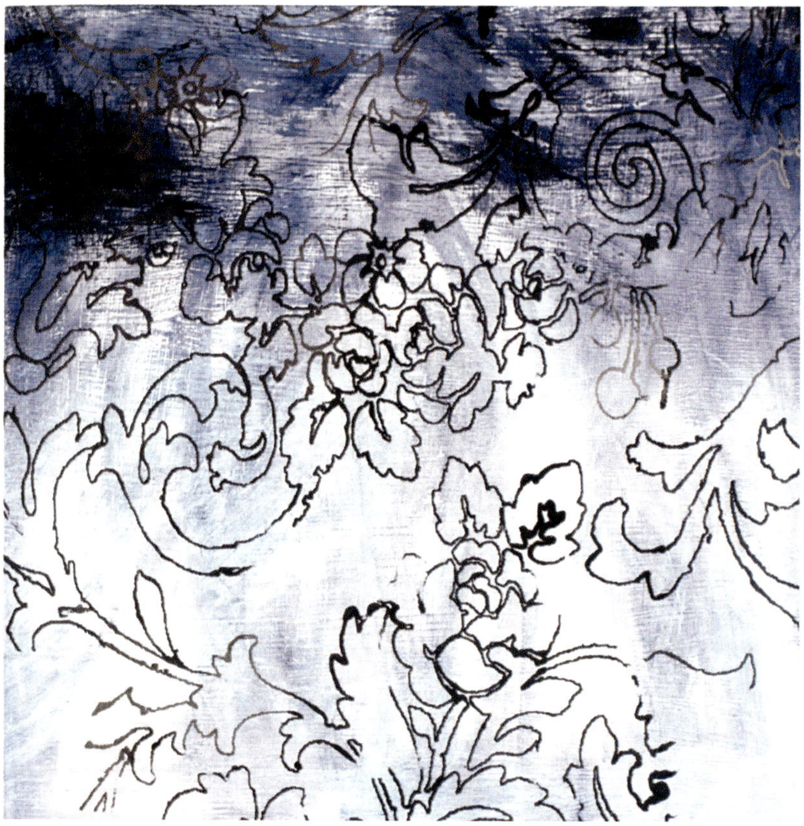

**Winsome Friend**
2002
oil, enamel, and acrylic on panel
17" x 17"
Collection of Loan Pham, New York

*bottom,* **Nightshade**
2001
oil and acrylic on panel
17" x 17"
Collection of Mary Kathryn Brown, Arkansas

*oopposite,* **Wild Card**
2003
oil, enamel, and acrylic on canvas
56" x 40 "
Collection of Bruce and Naomi Usher, New York

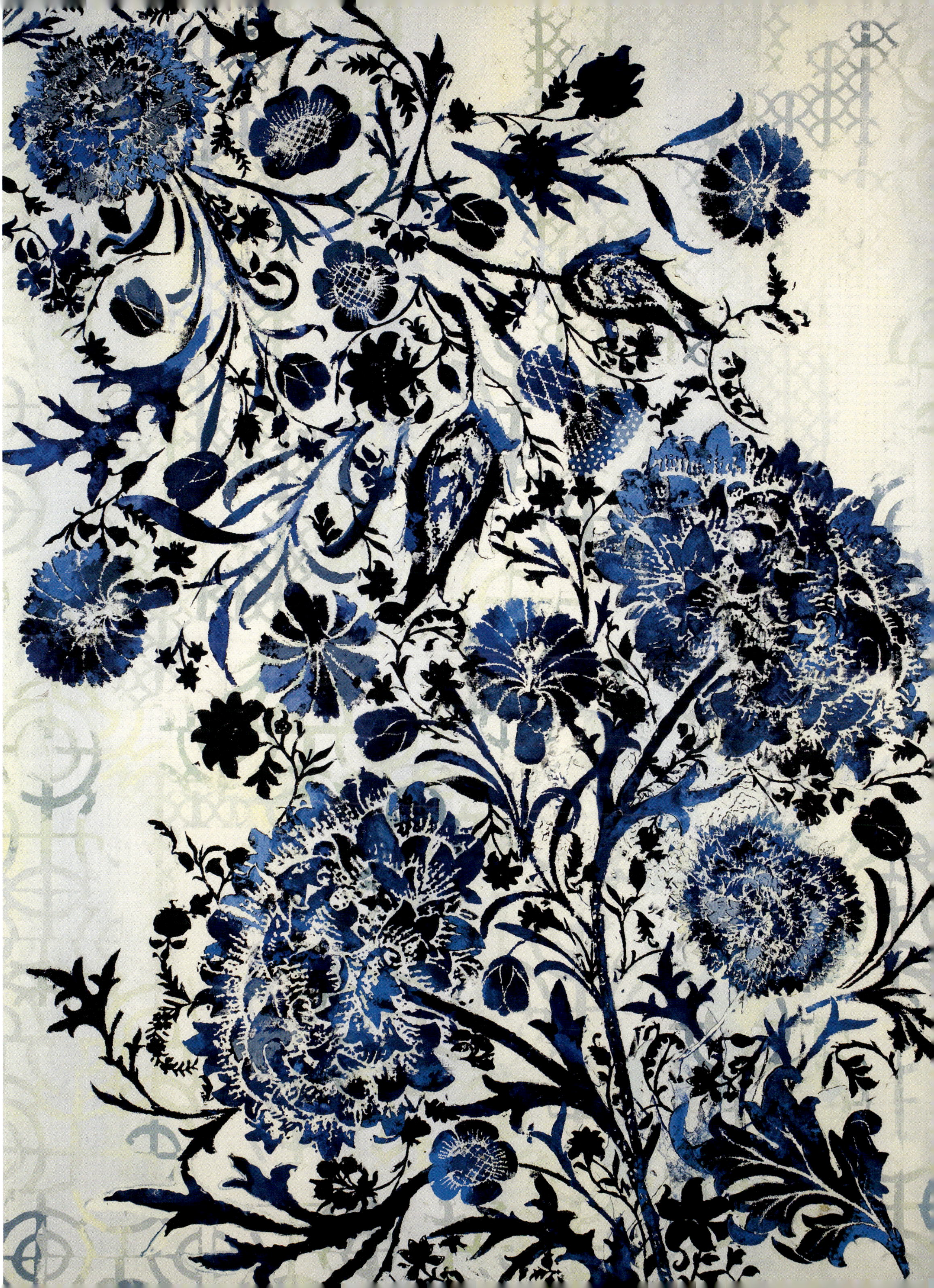

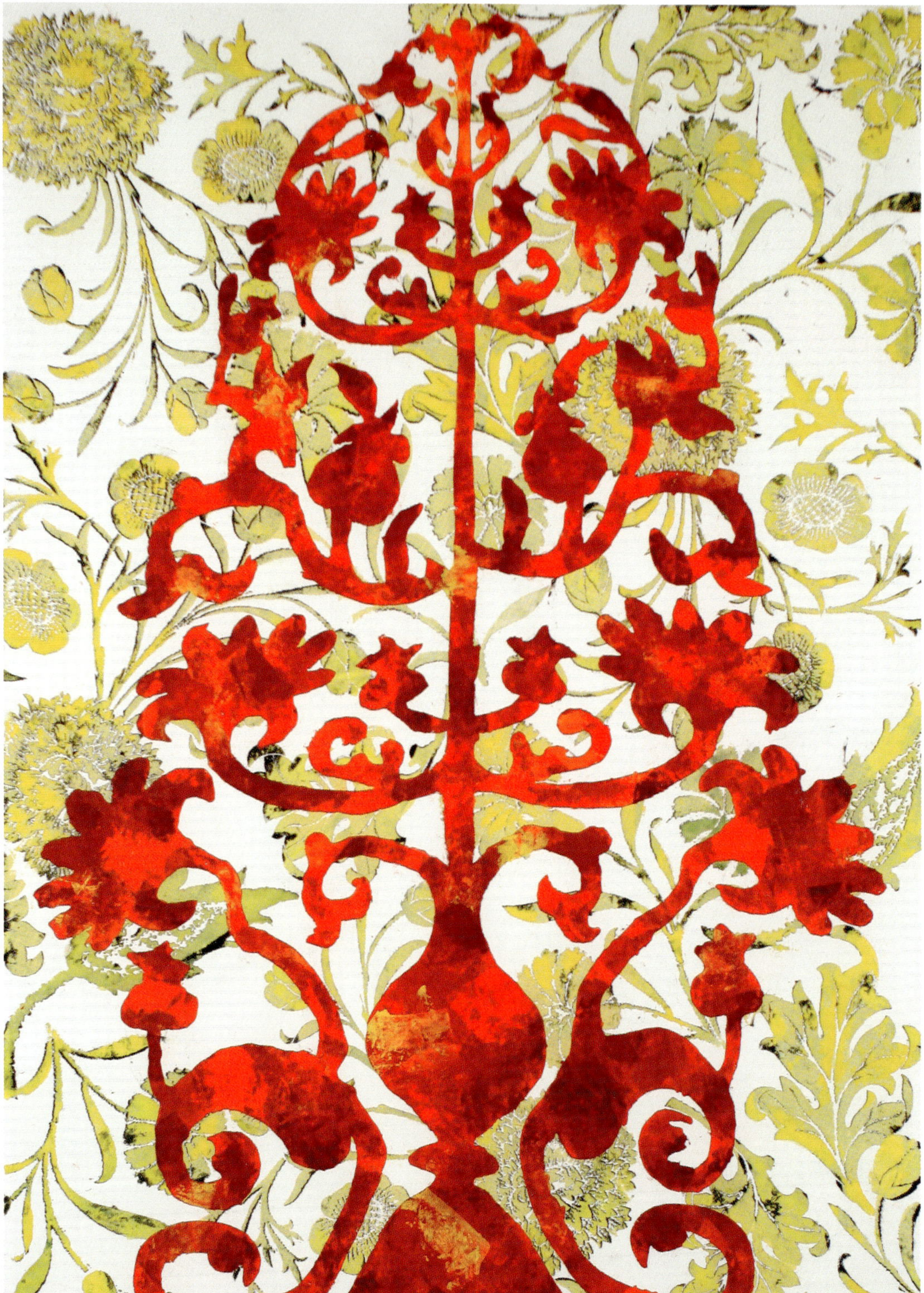

**Cultural Instruction I**

2004

oil, enamel, and acrylic on canvas

56" x 40"

Collection of Natasha & Ross Taylor, Australia

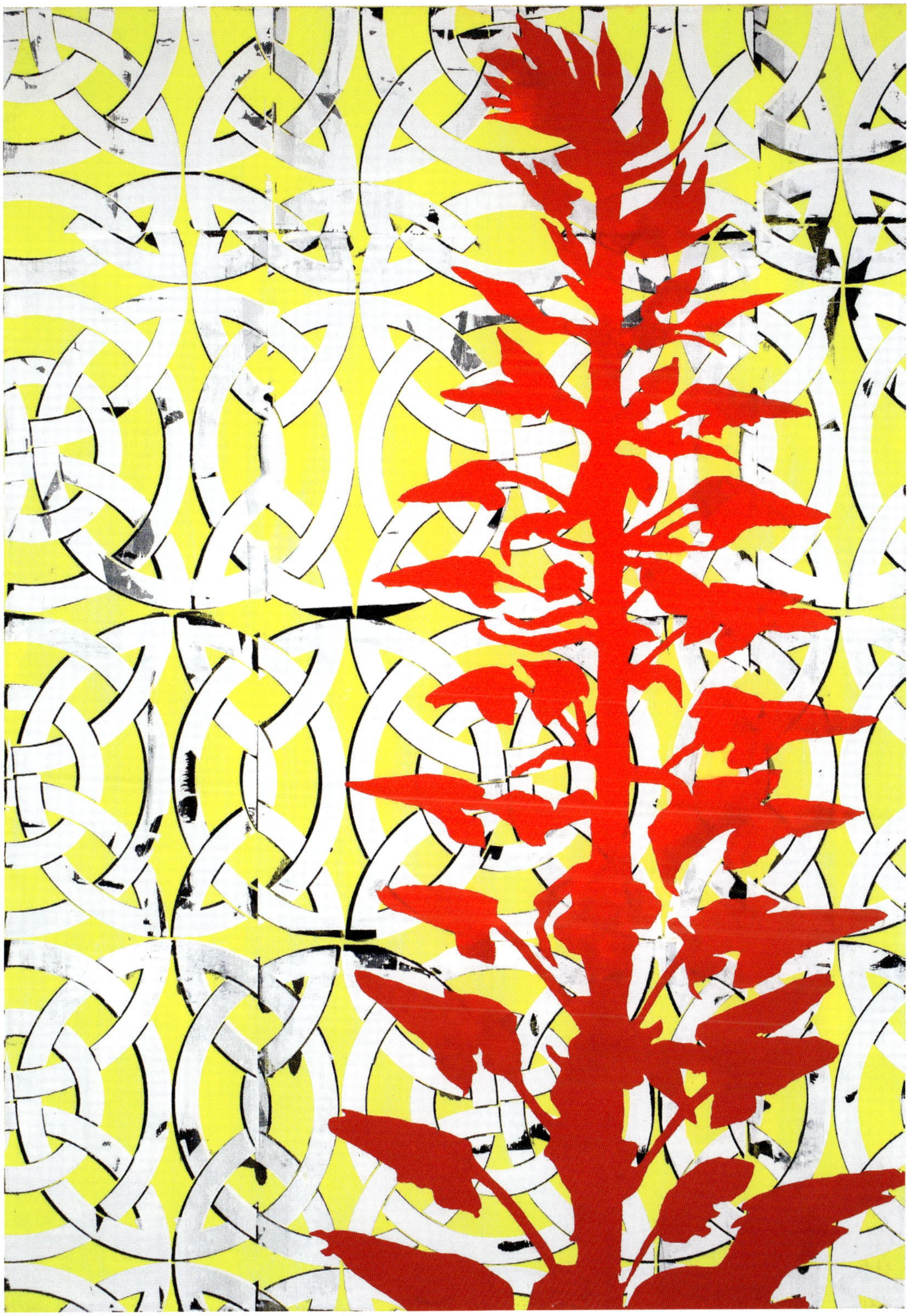

**The Same Winter**

2008

oil, acrylic, and enamel on canvas

56" x 40"

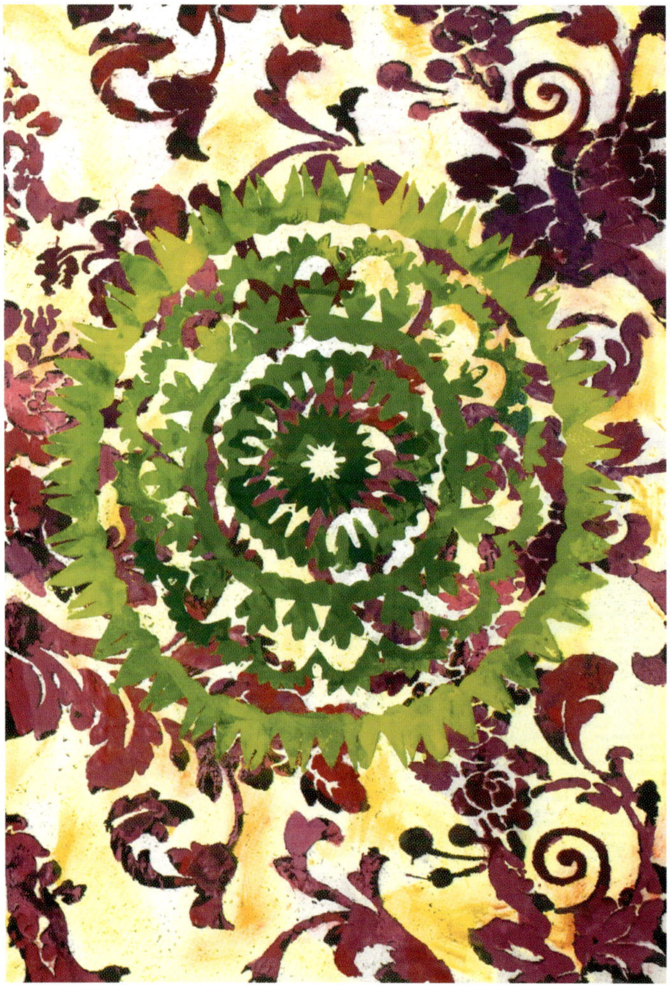

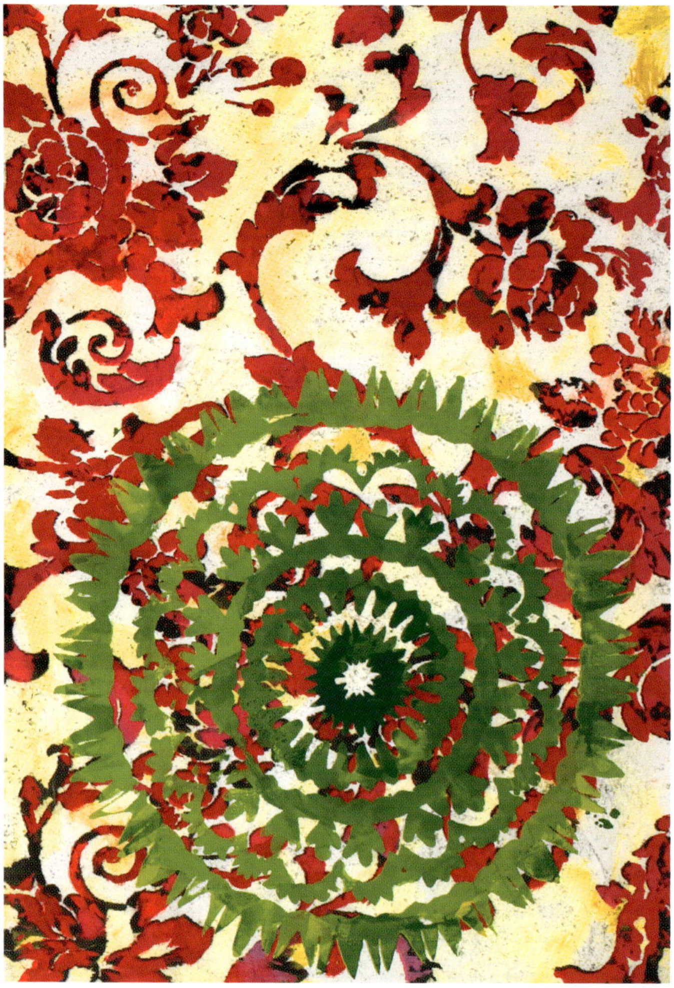

**Midsummer's Marriage I (Tippett)**
**Midsummer's Marriage II (Tippett)**
2004
oil, enamel, acrylic, and pigmented pulp on paper
each work: 36" x 25"
Collection of Bill and Jodi Gorin, New York

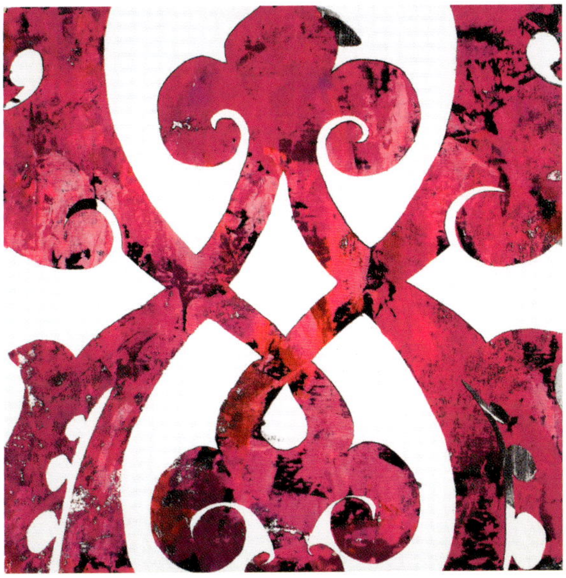

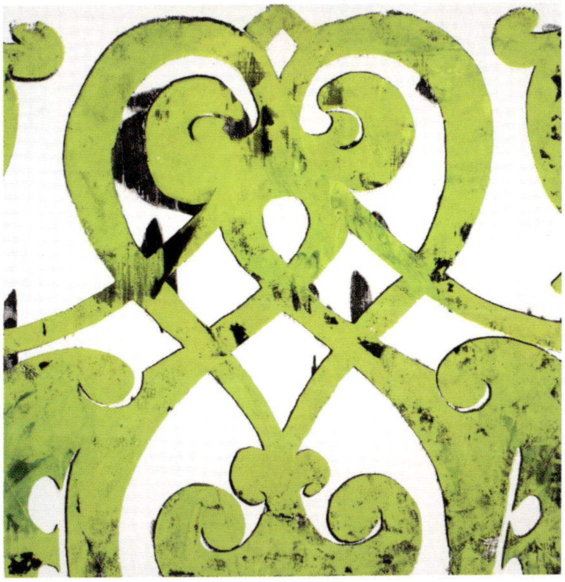

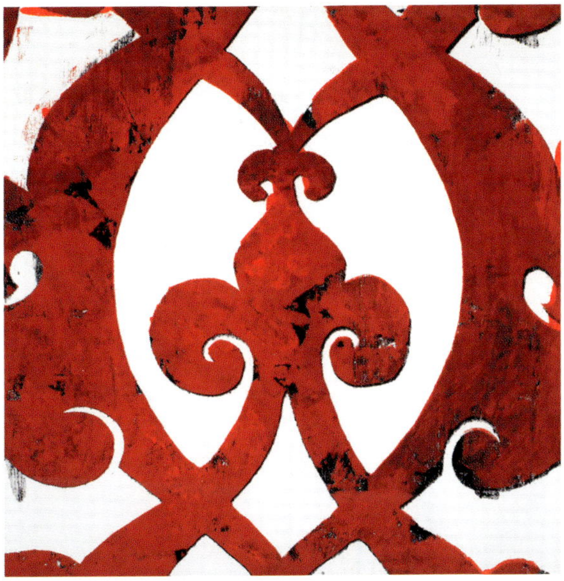

**Tattoo (magenta)**
2004
oil and enamel on panel
21" x 21"

**Tattoo (green)**
2004
oil and enamel on panel
21" x 21"

**Tattoo (red)**
2004
oil and enamel on panel
21" x 21"
Collection of Pamela Butler, New York

**Lust Card**
2005
oil and acrylic on canvas
56" x 40"

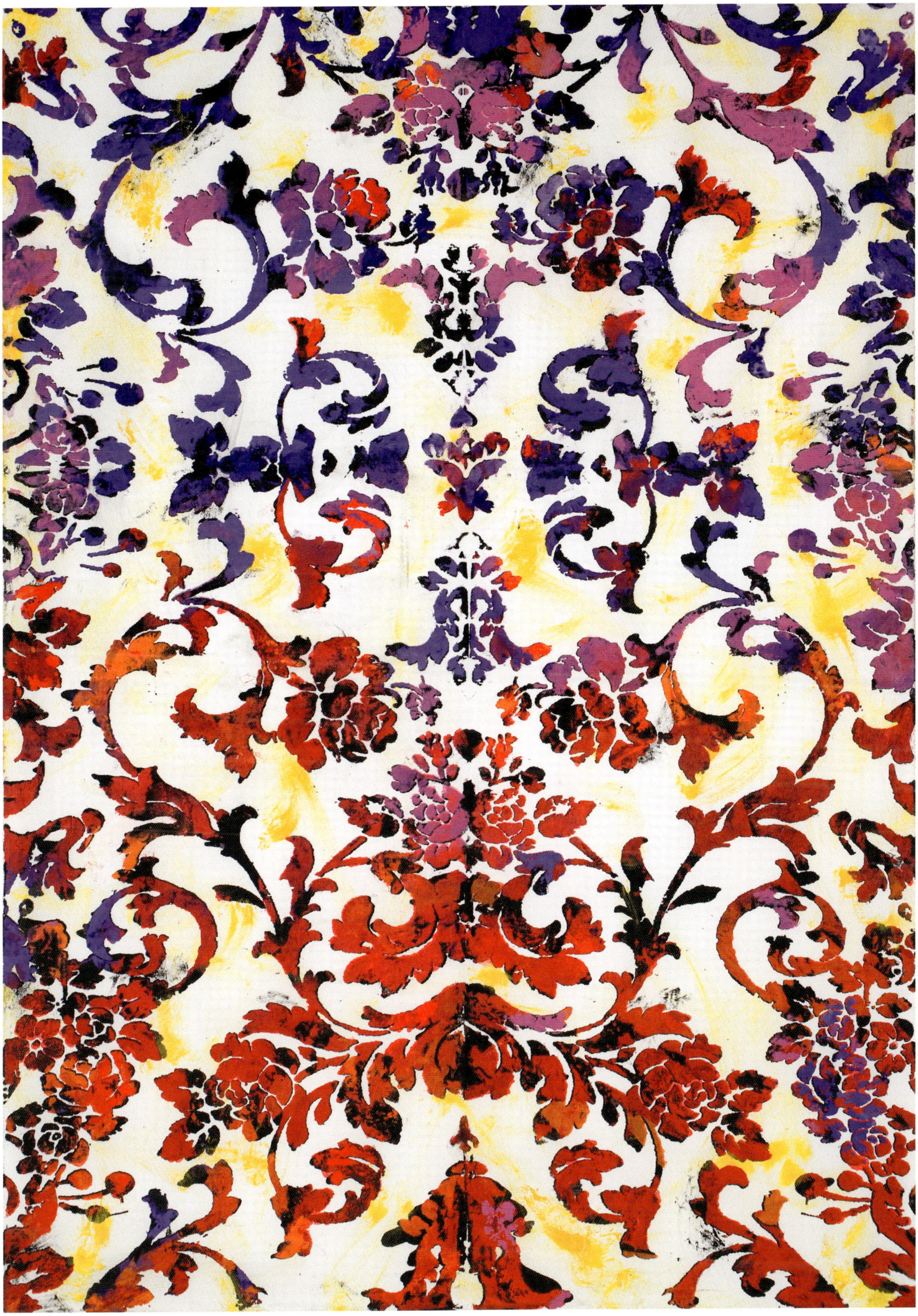

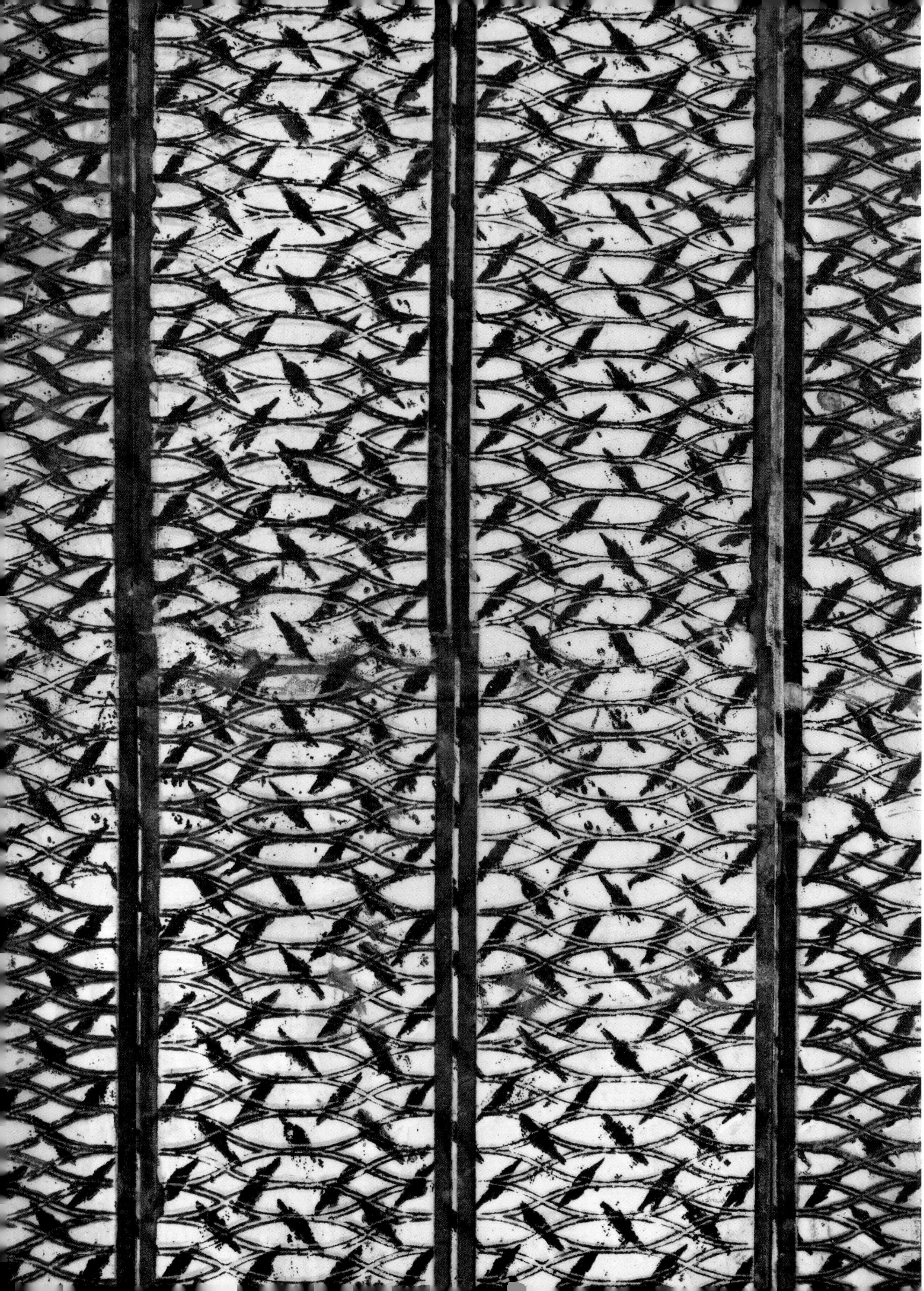

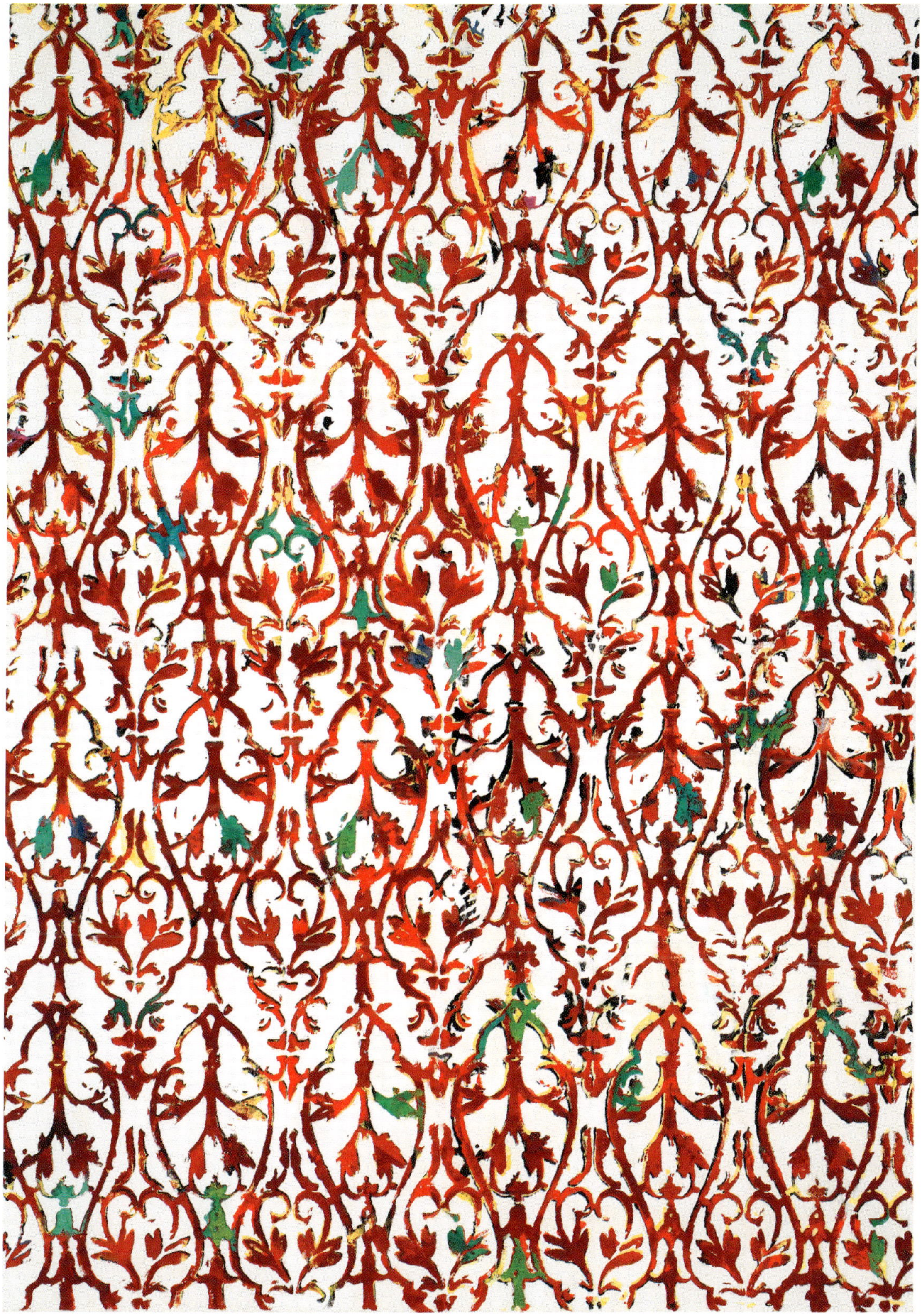

**Ambidextrous**
2004
oil, enamel, and acrylic on canvas
56" x 40 "

*opposite, detail:*
**U.T. (Wings)**
1997
acrylic on mylar
120" x 14"

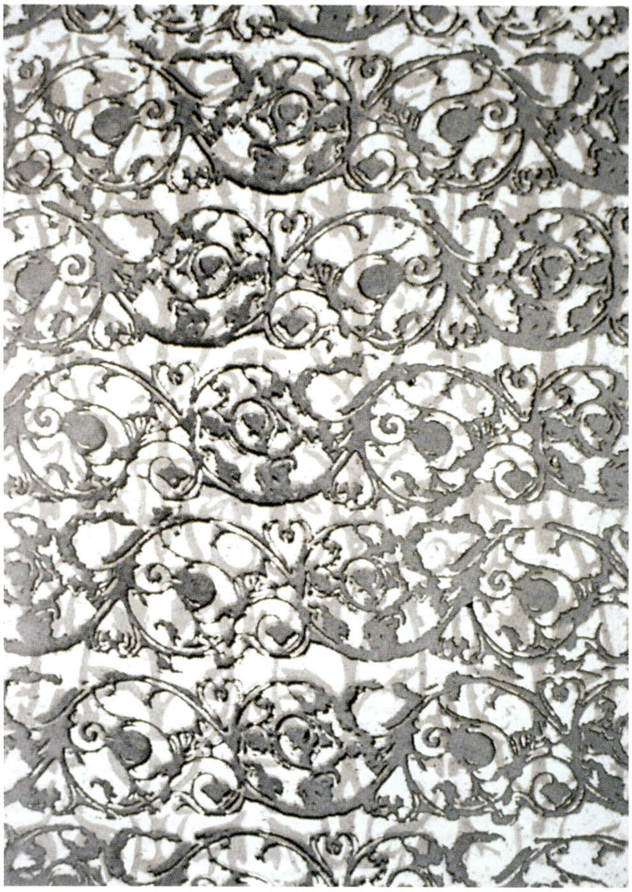

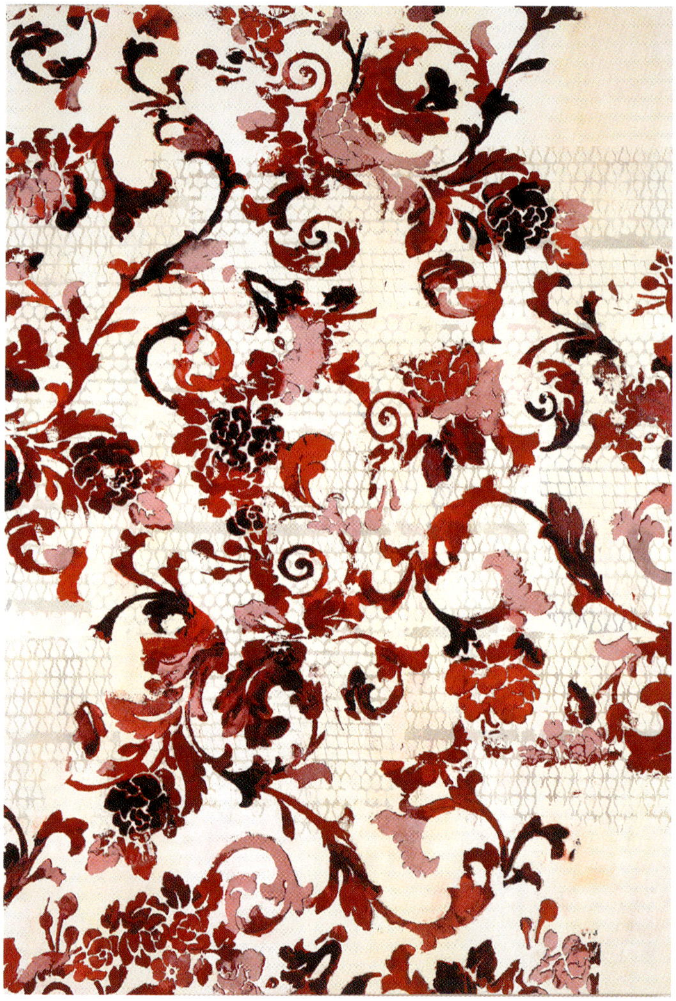

**Strangeness of Beauty**
1998-99
screenprinted paper pulp on cotton rag
30" x 22"
Collection of the Harvard Art Museums/
Fogg Museum"

*right,* **Juvenelia**
2004
oil, enamel, and acrylic on canvas
56" x 40"

*opposite,* **Broken Serenade**
2000
acrylic on mylar on panel
14" x 14"
Collection of Jean-Yves Noblet, New York

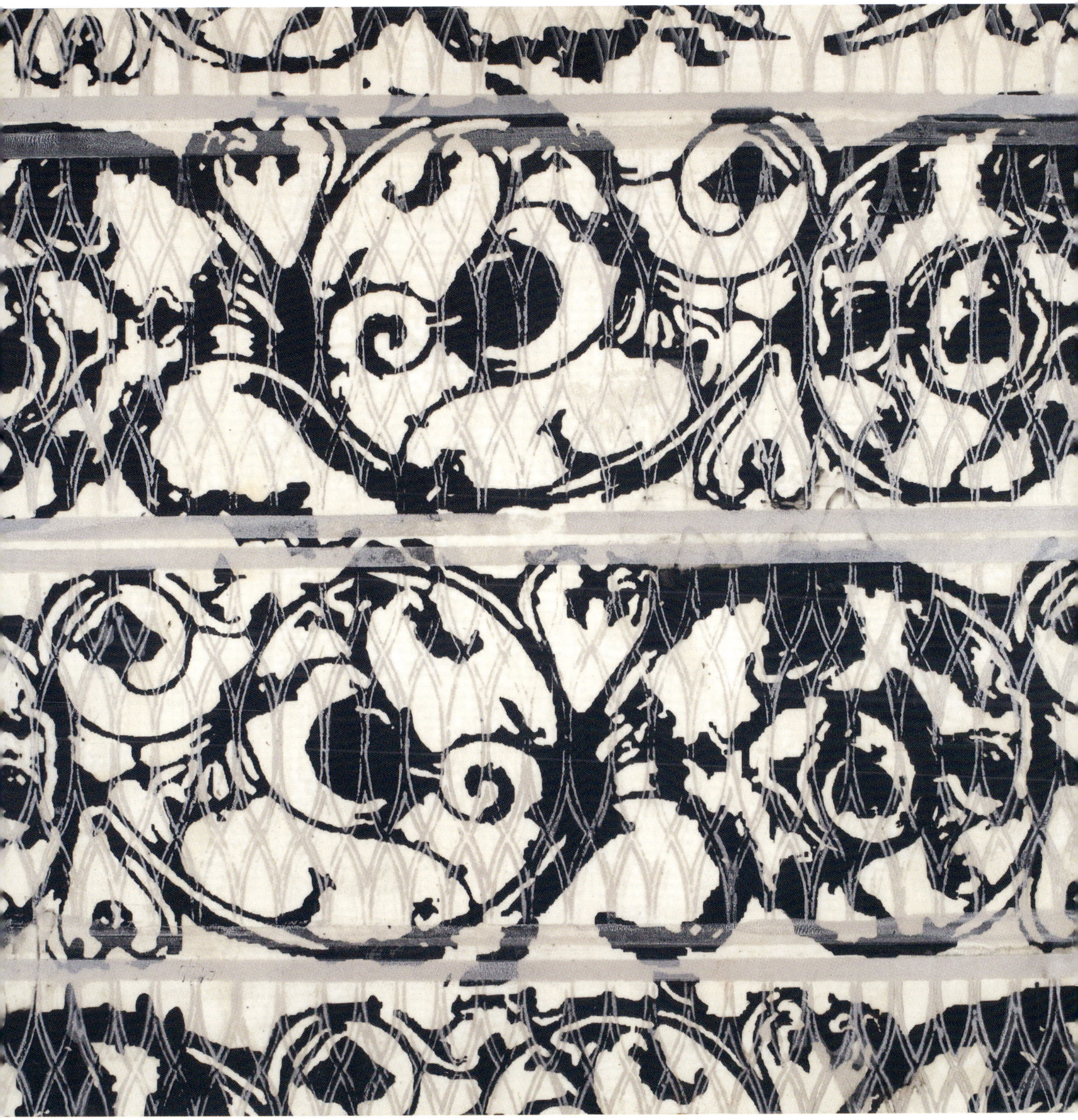

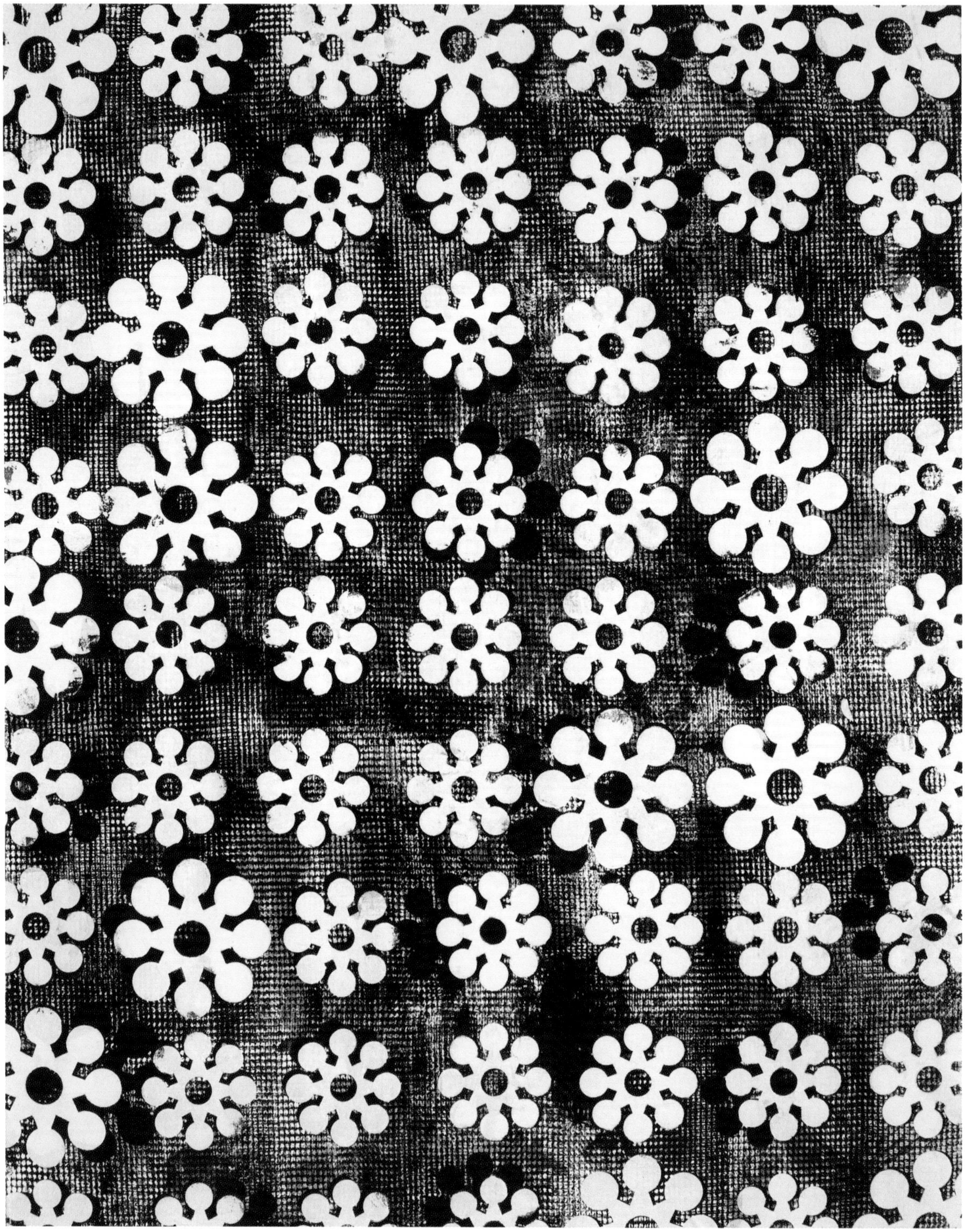

**It's All Spiritual**
2008
oil, enamel, and acrylic on canvas
60" x 52"

*opposite,* **Distant Theatres**
2006
enamel and acrylic on canvas mounted to wall, site specific installation for the Bernard Toale Gallery, Boston
144" x 120"

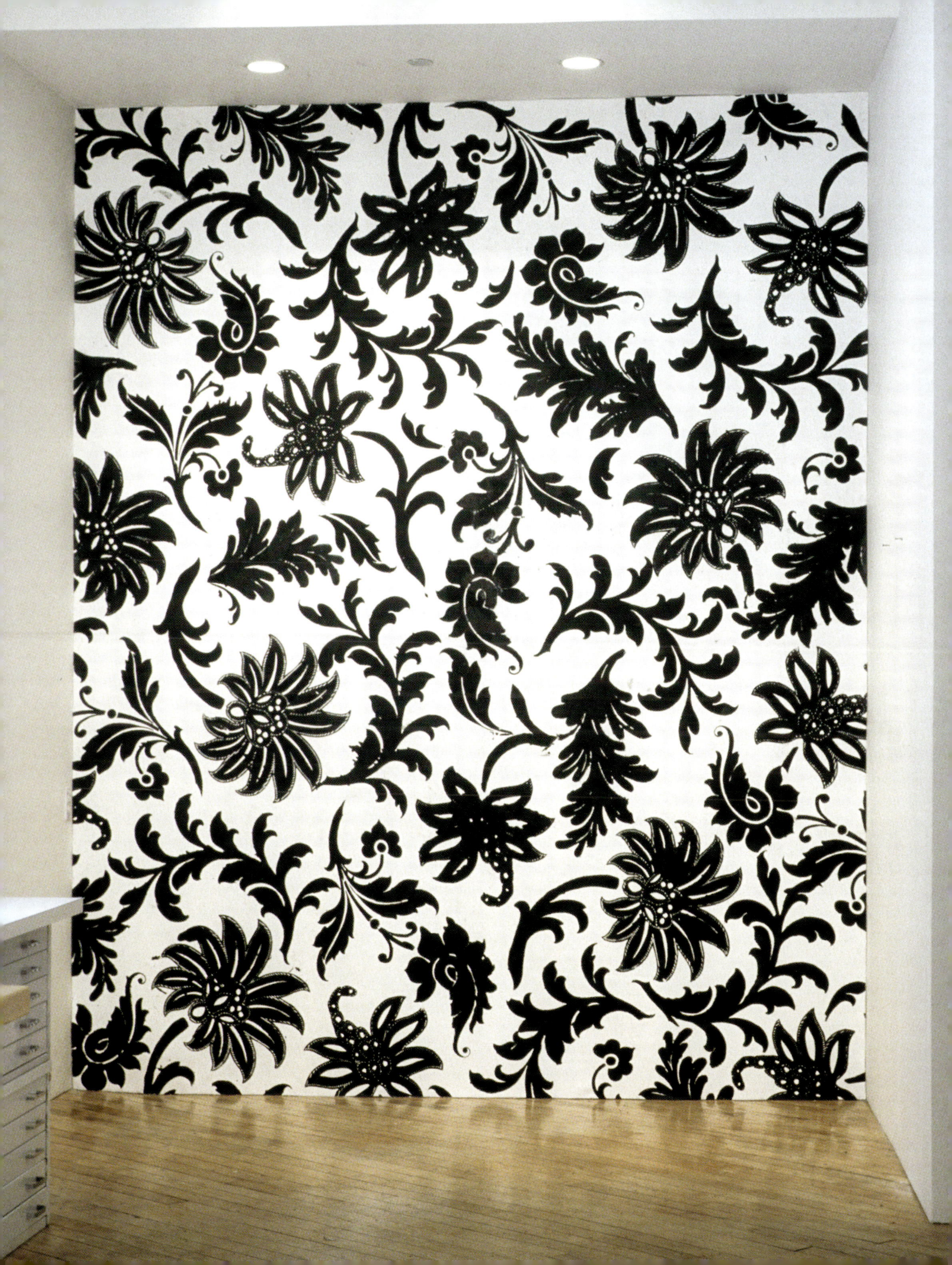

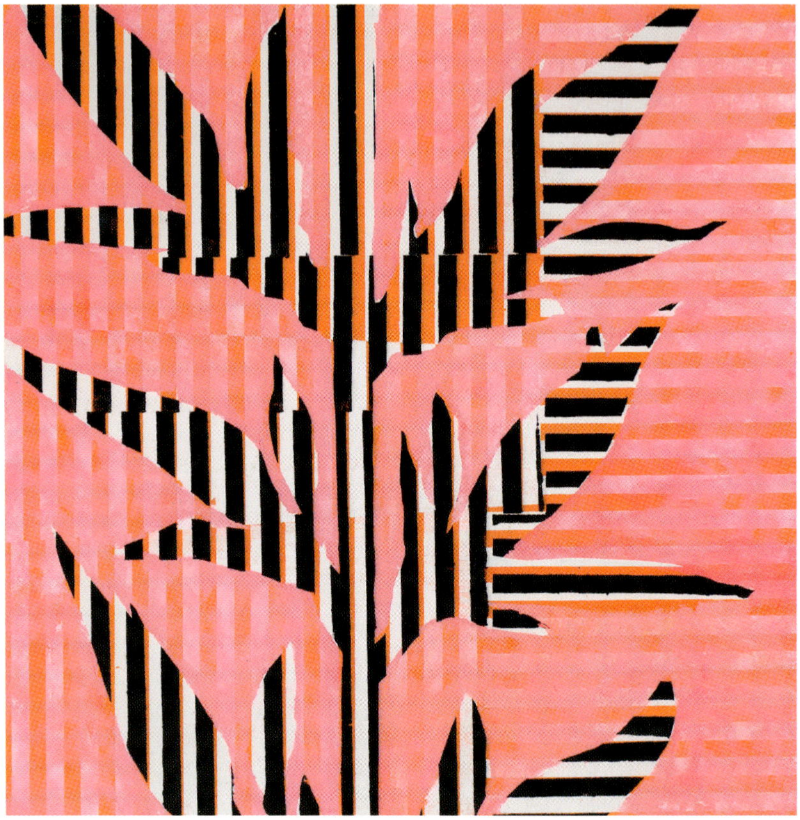

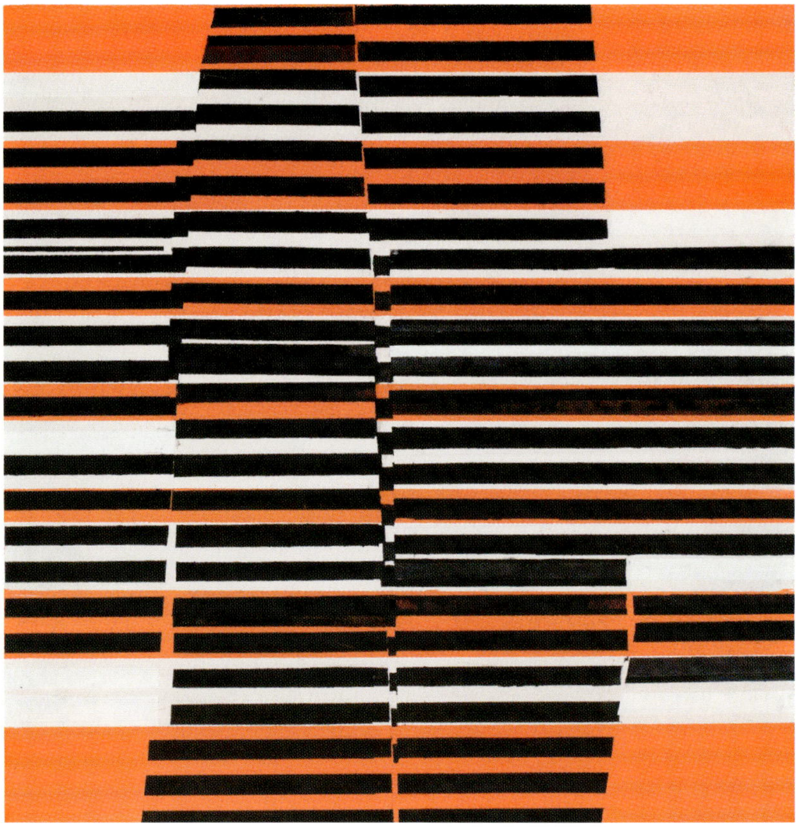

**Belur 0832**
2009
oil and enamel on panel
24" x 24"

*bottom,* **Musiri 0432**
2009
oil and enamel on panel
24" x 24"

*opposite,* **Signal Jumping, Black**
2010
oil, acrylic, and enamel on canvas
56" x 40"

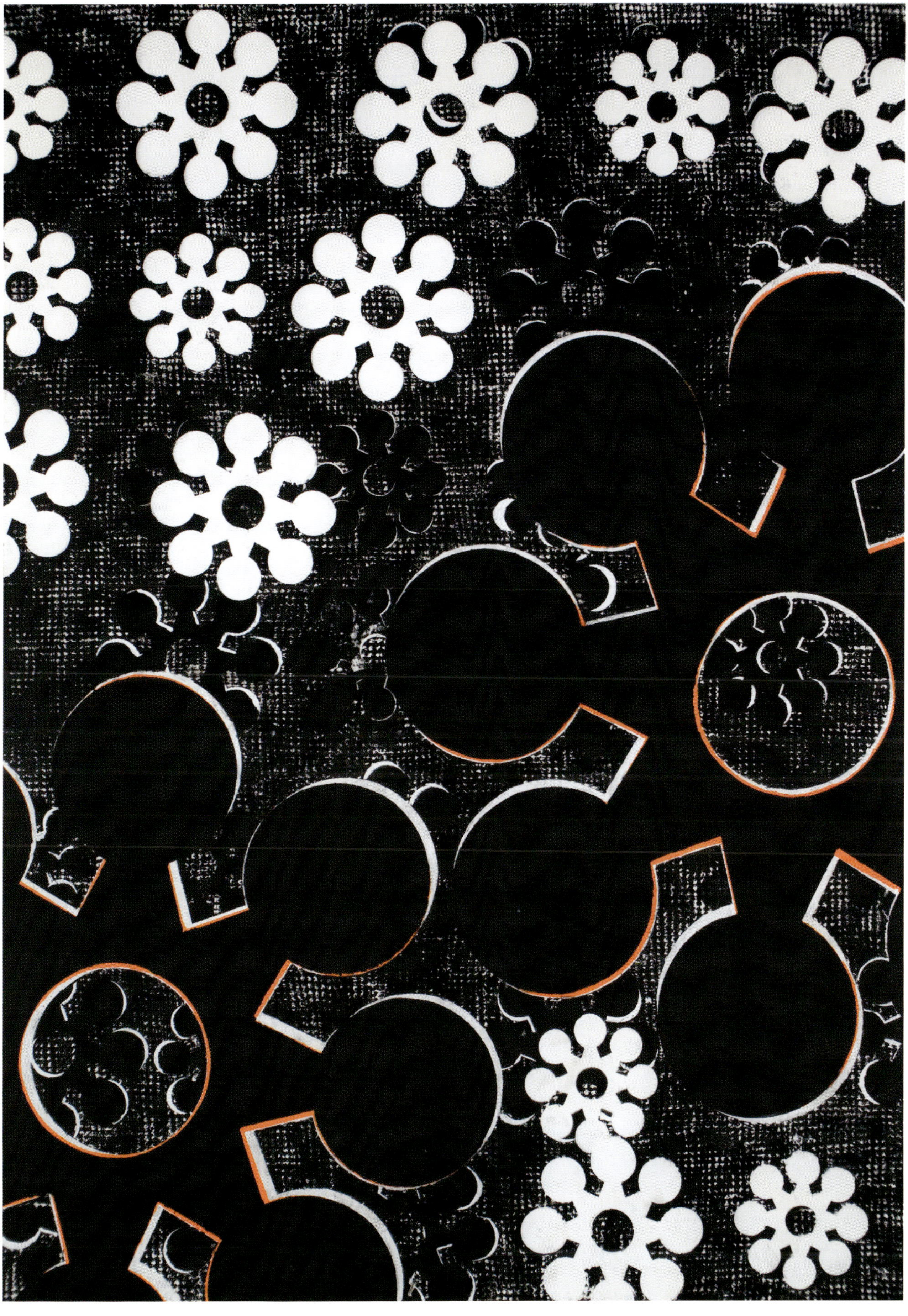

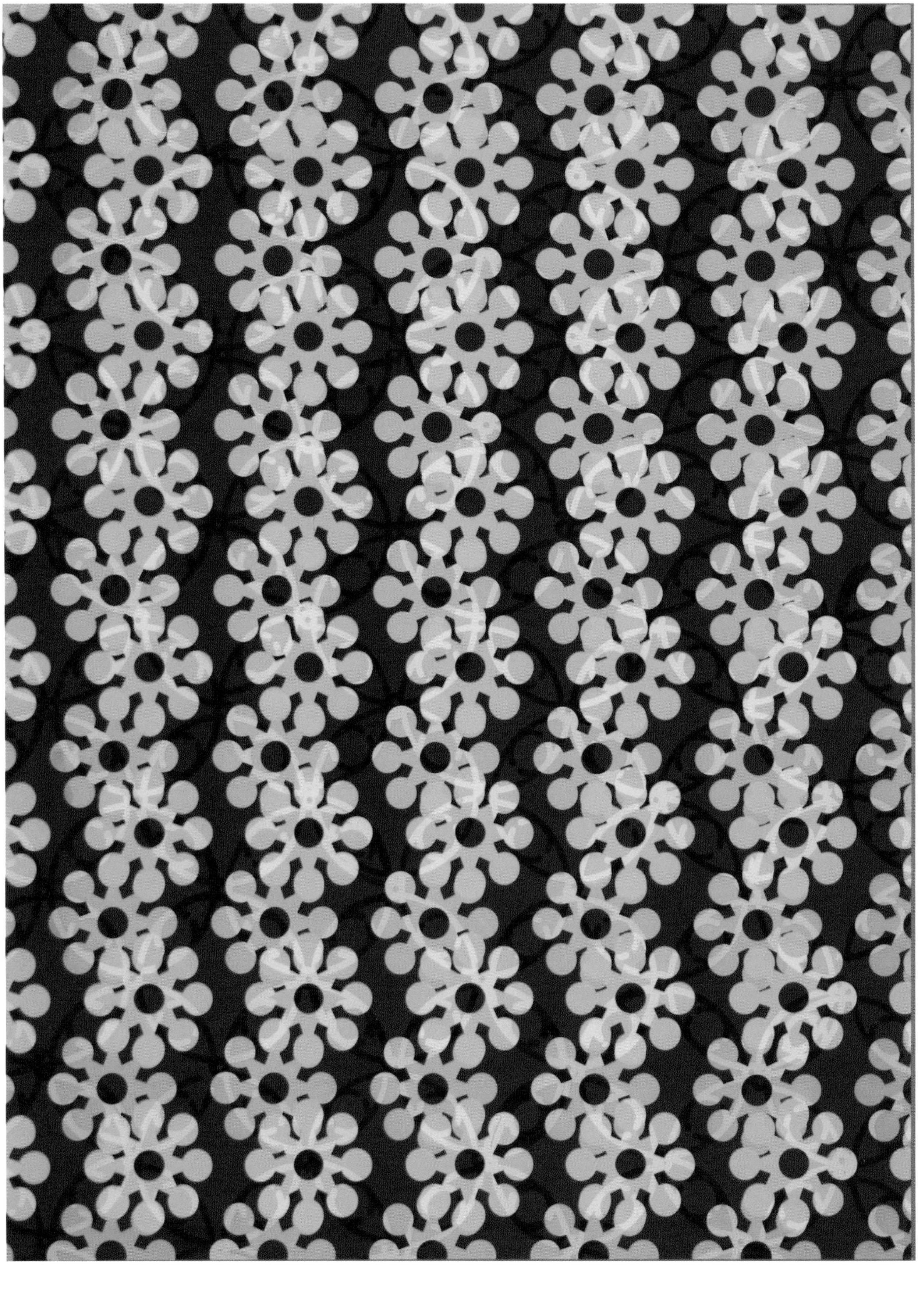

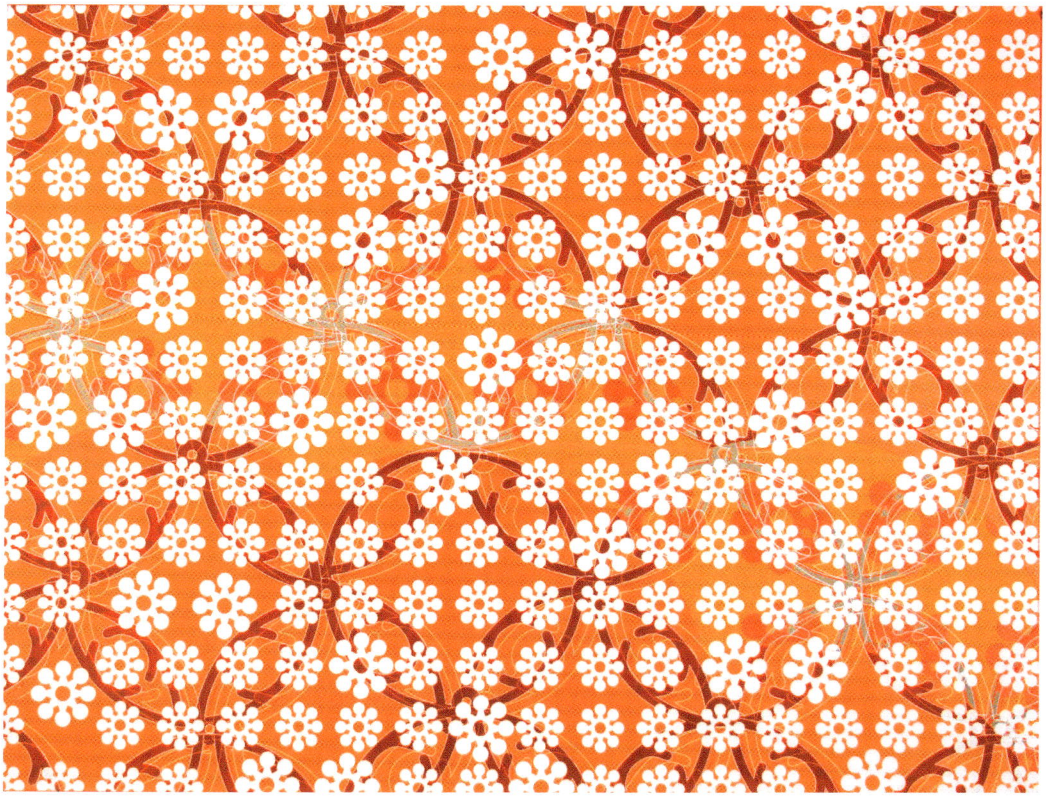

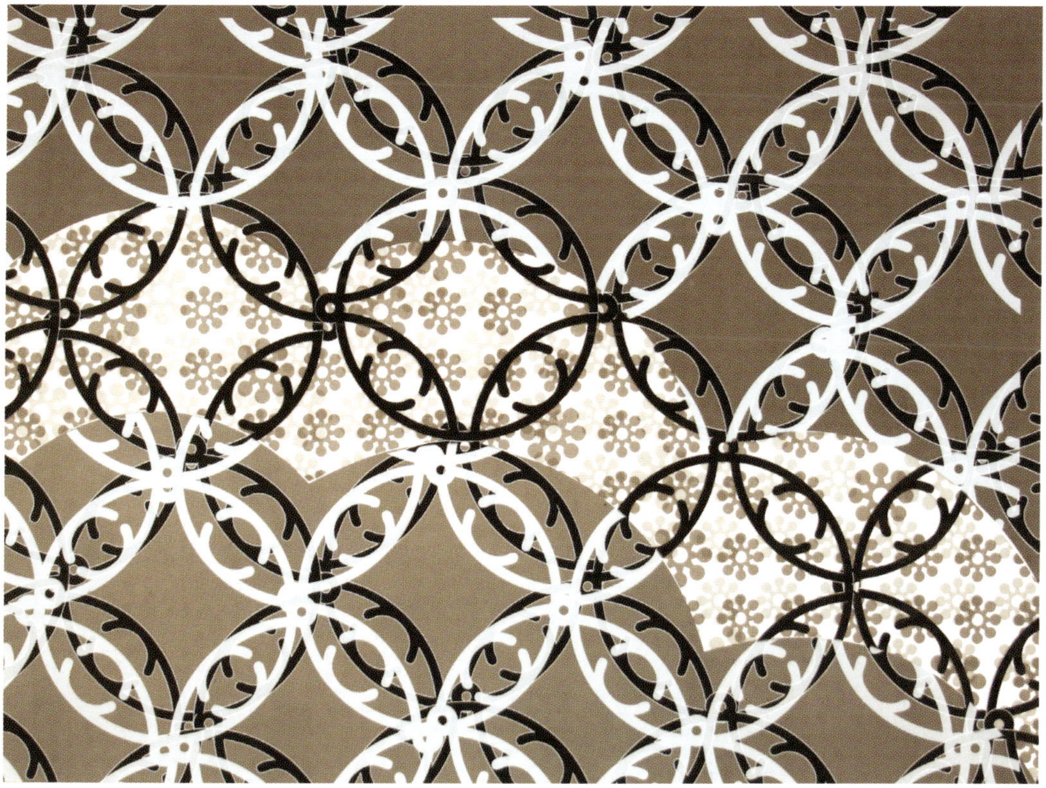

**Echolalia, The Forgetting of Language N. 3**
2007
acrylic on paper, unique screenprint
33" x 44"

*bottom,* **Echolalia, The Forgetting of Language N. 4**
2007
acrylic on paper, unique screenprint
33" x 44"

*opposite,* **Echolalia, The Forgetting of Language N. 15**
2007
acrylic on paper, unique screenprint
44" x 33"

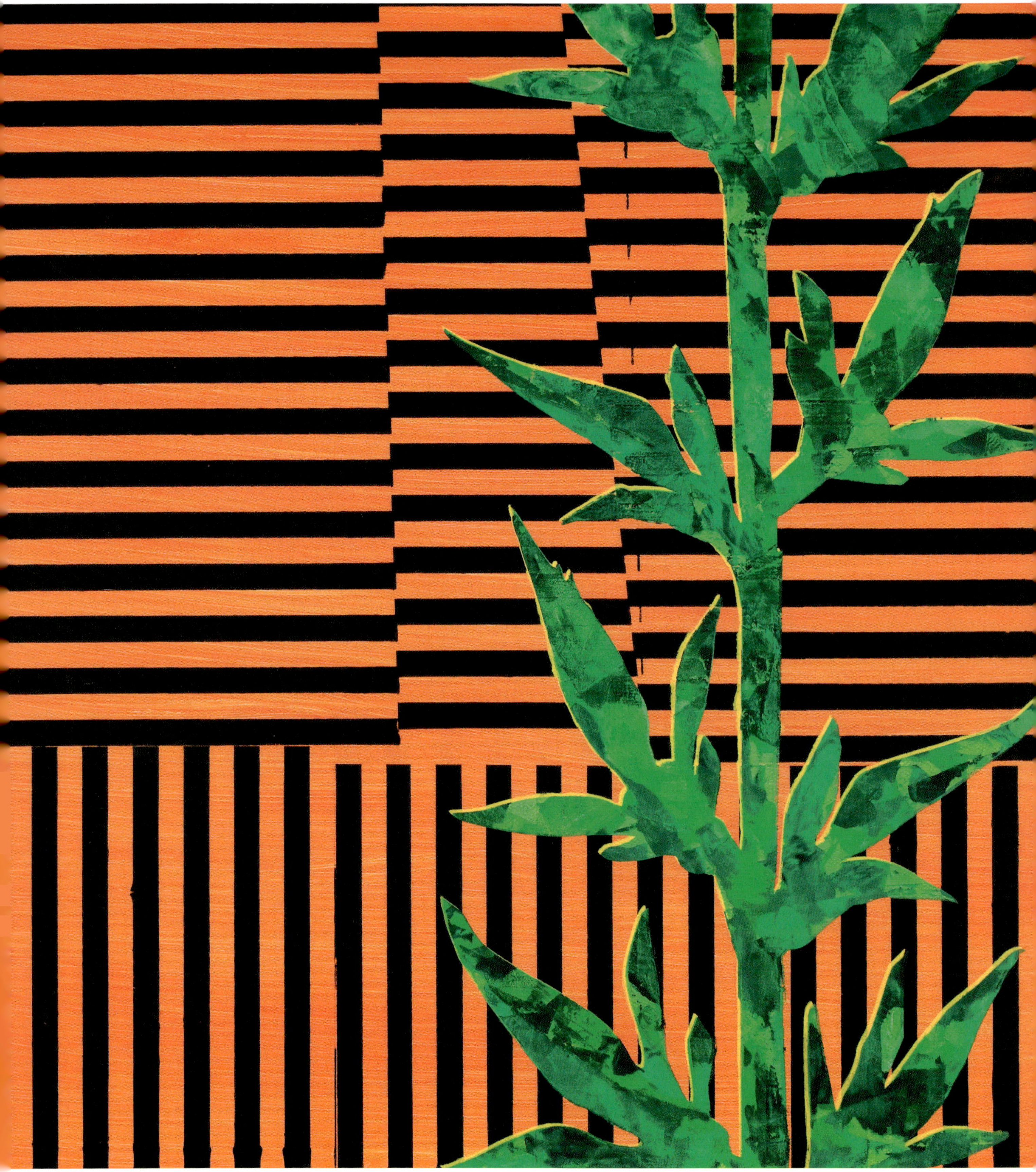

**Indore 0731**
2009
oil and enamel on panel
24" x 24"

*opposite,* **Beed 0244**
2009
oil and enamel on panel
24" x 24"

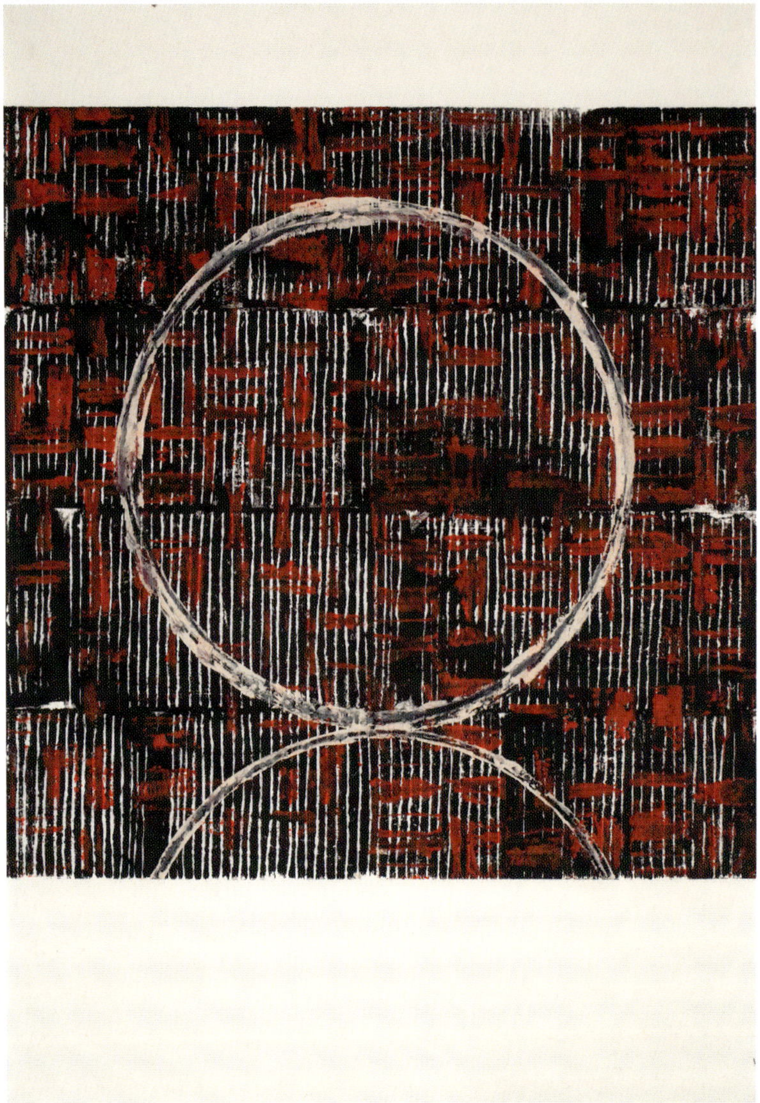

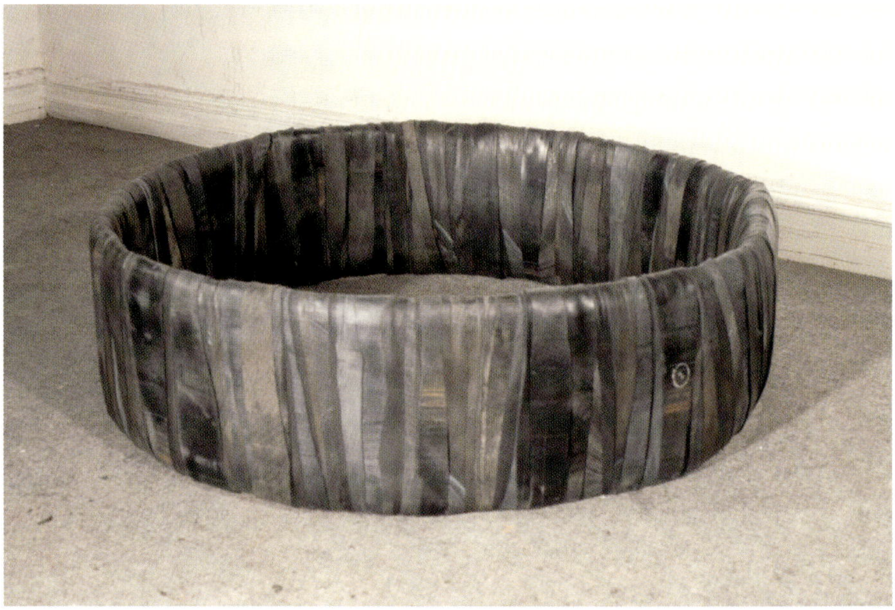

**Untitled (head)**
1992
ink on paper
40" x 28"

*right,* **Bandgare**
1990
rubber over board
26" x 60" diameter
Private Collection, Cologne, Germany

*opposite,* **Last Two Million**
2008
oil, enamel, and acrylic on canvas
60" x 52"

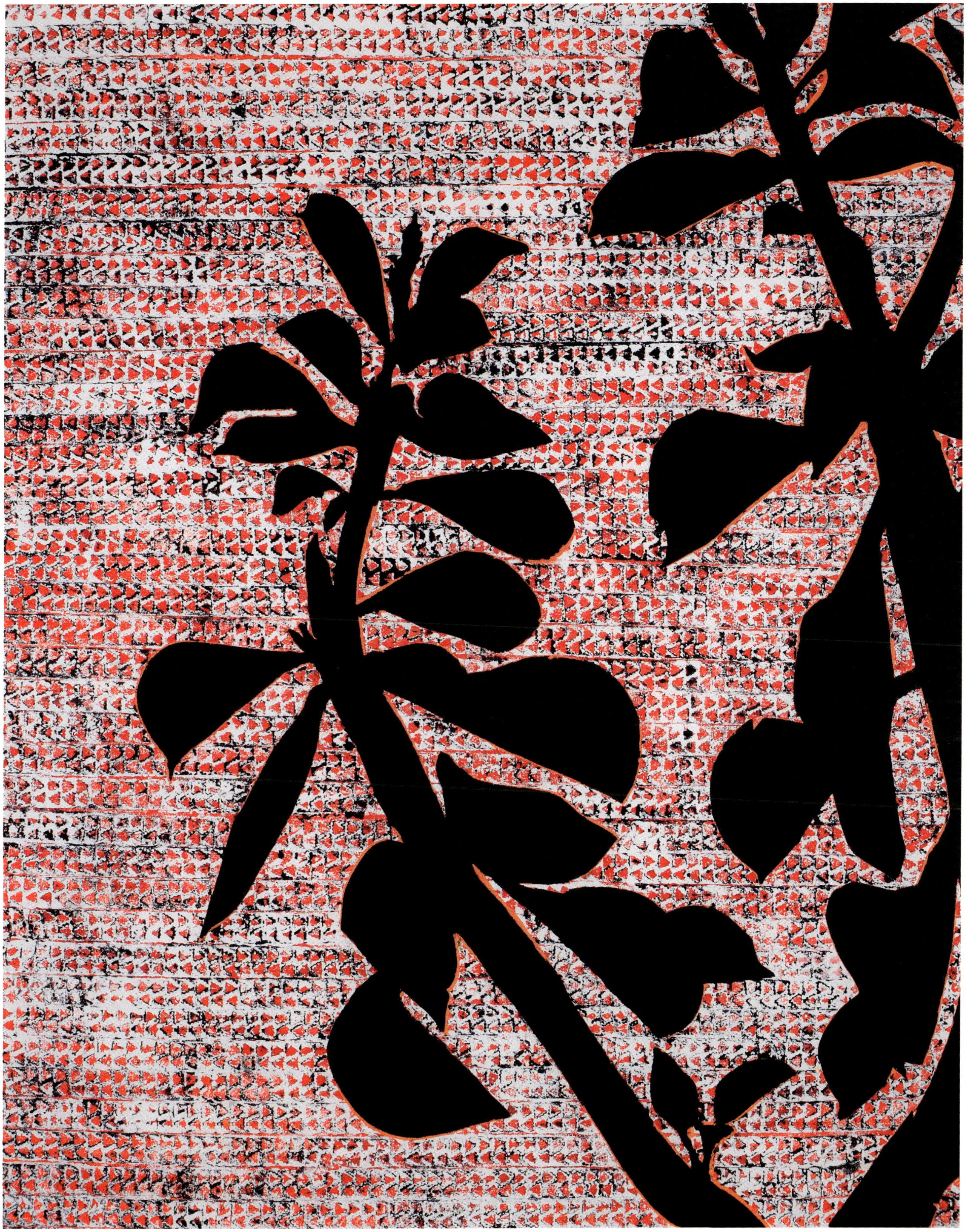

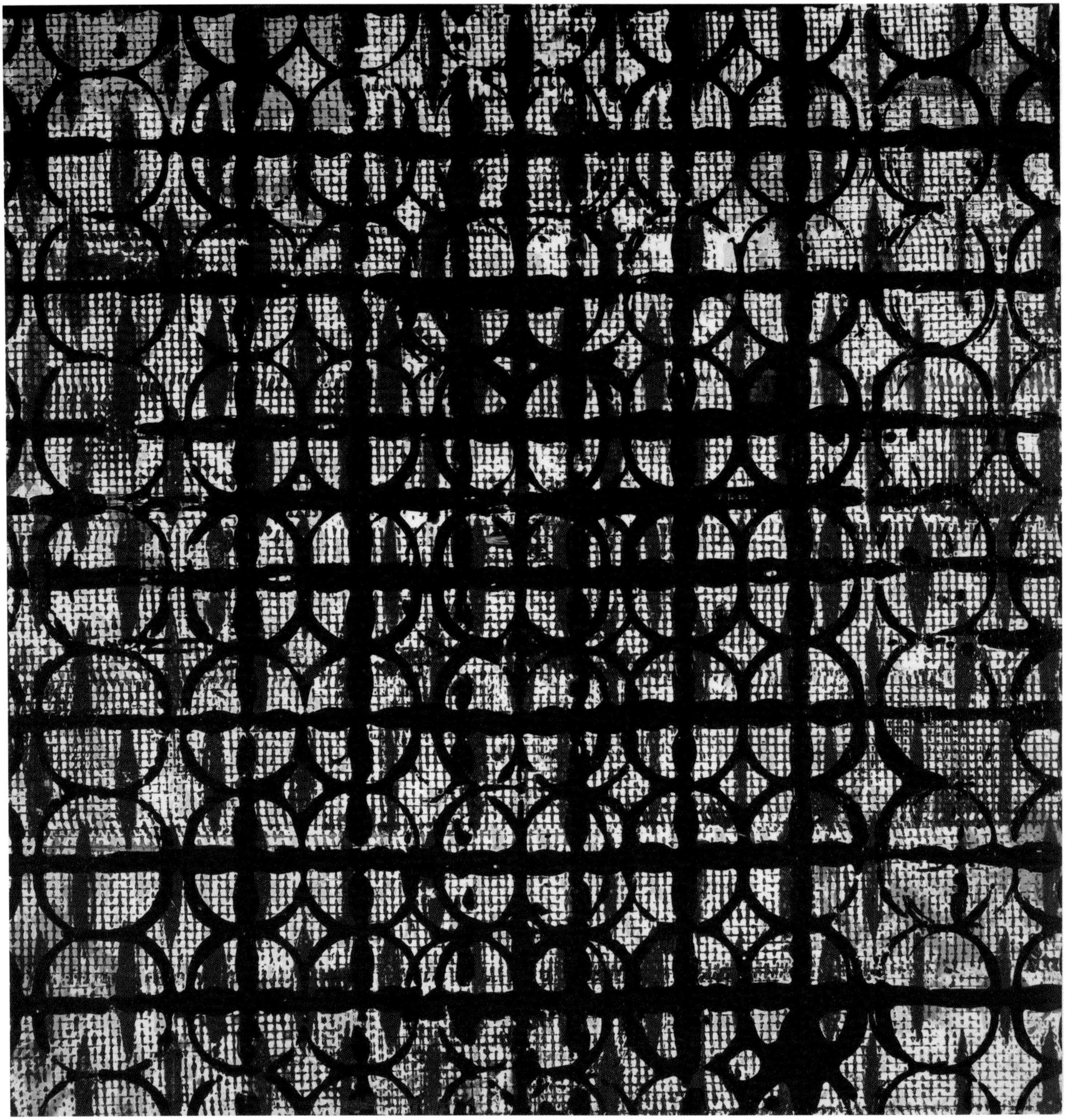

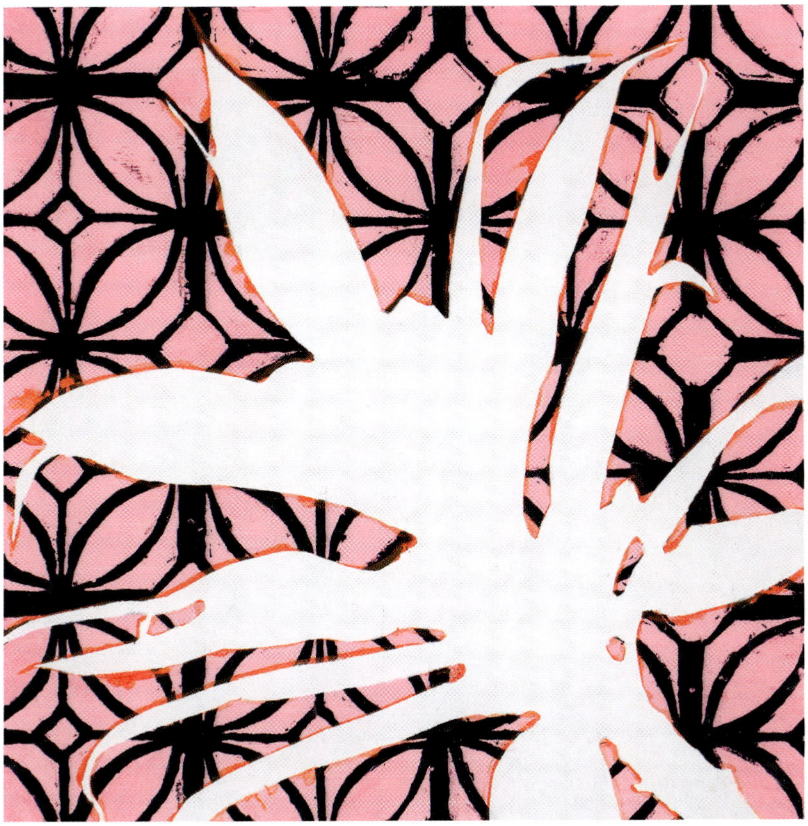

*left,* **Biophilia: Eve**
2007
oil and enamel on panel
22" x 22"

*below,* **Echolalia, The Forgetting of Language N. 2**
2007
acrylic on paper, unique screenprint
33" x 44"
Collection of Jean-Yves Noblet

*opposite,* **Dreamless**
2000
acrylic and enamel on mylar on panel
14" x 14"
Collection of Niall Worn, Germany

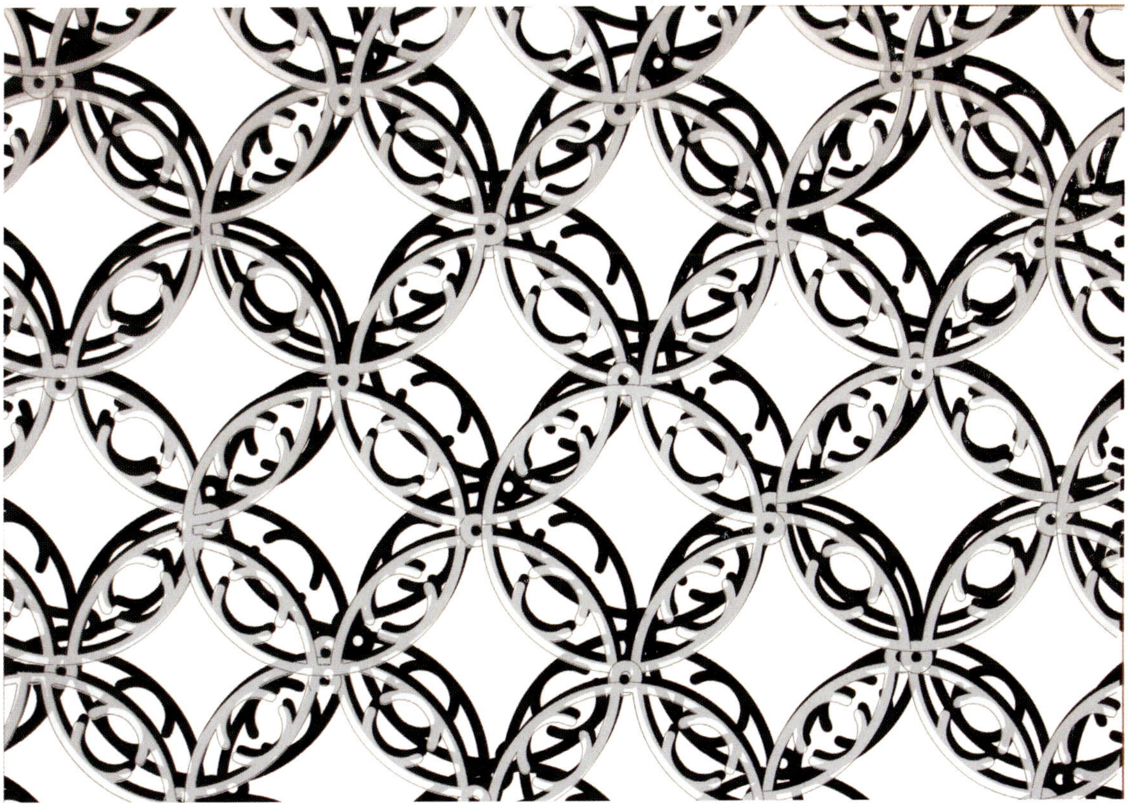

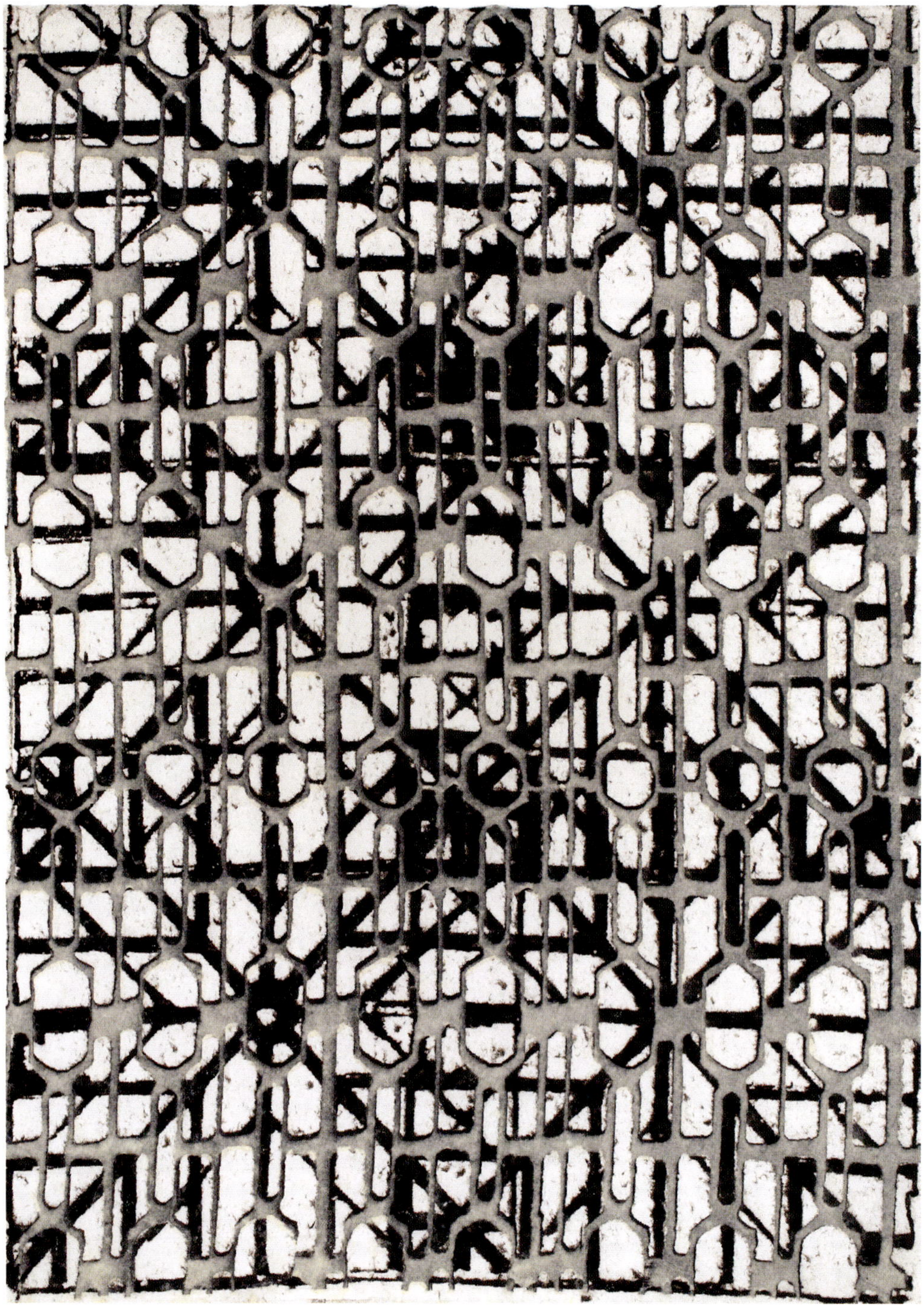

**Night Map**
1998-99
screenprinted paper pulp on
cotton rag
30" x 22"
Collection of Niall Worn, Germany

*opposite,*
**Jorhat 0376**
2009
oil and enamel on panel
24" x 24"

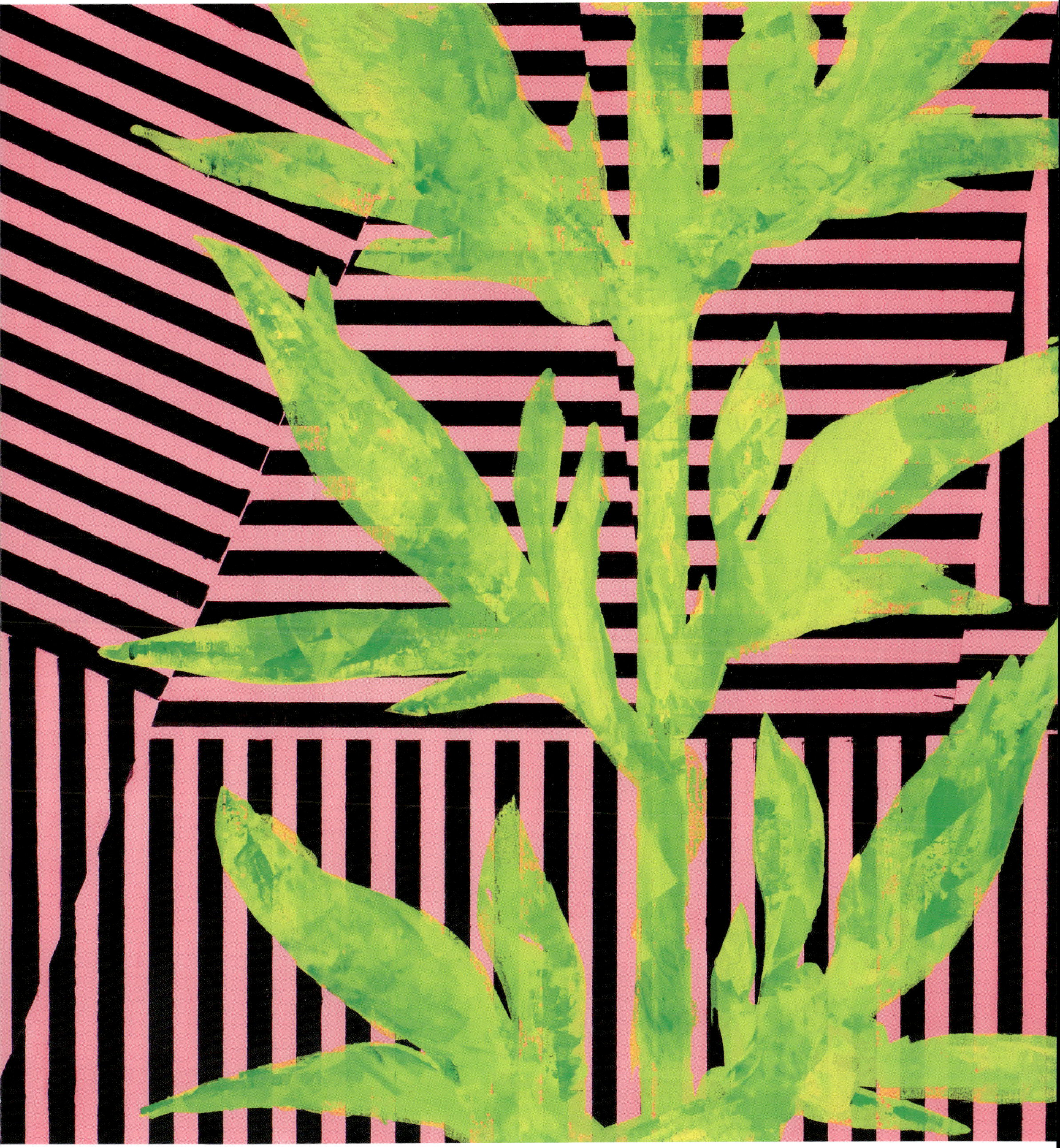

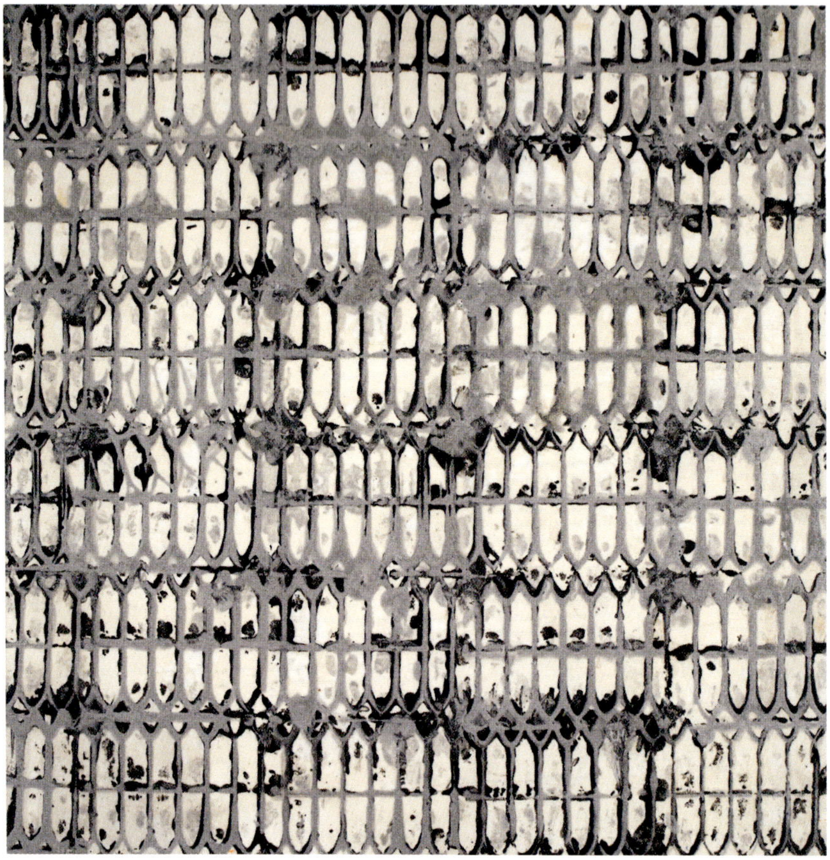

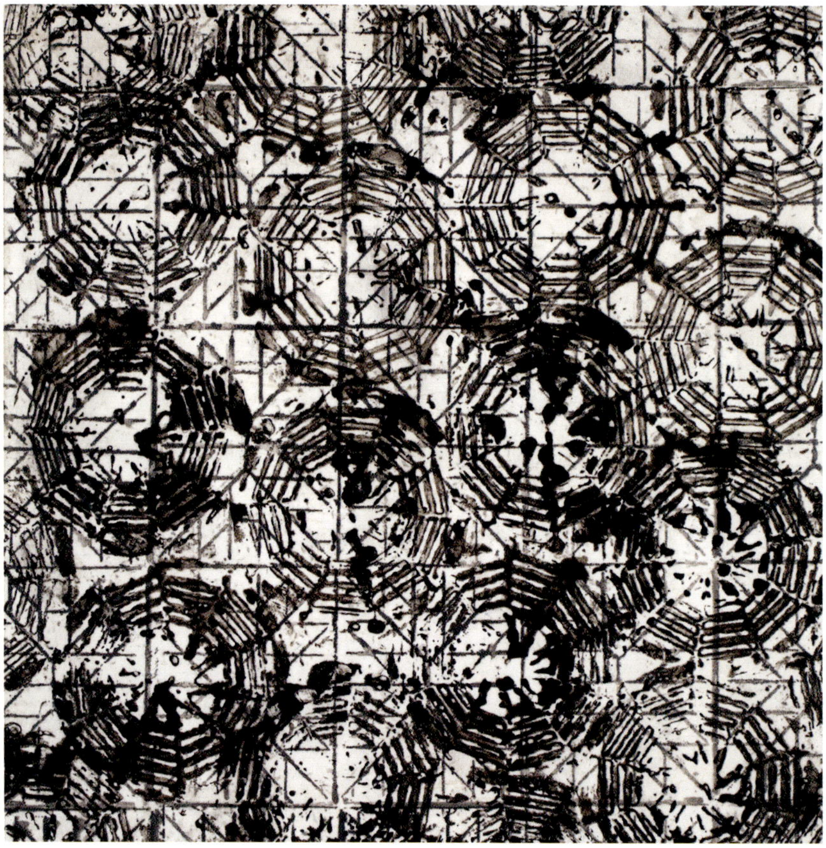

**Tracery**
1991-98
acrylic and polyurethane on
mylar on panel
14" x 14"

*bottom,* **Science Punk**
1998
acrylic and polyurethane on
mylar on panel
14" x 14"
On loan to Daryl Isaacs, M.D.,
New York

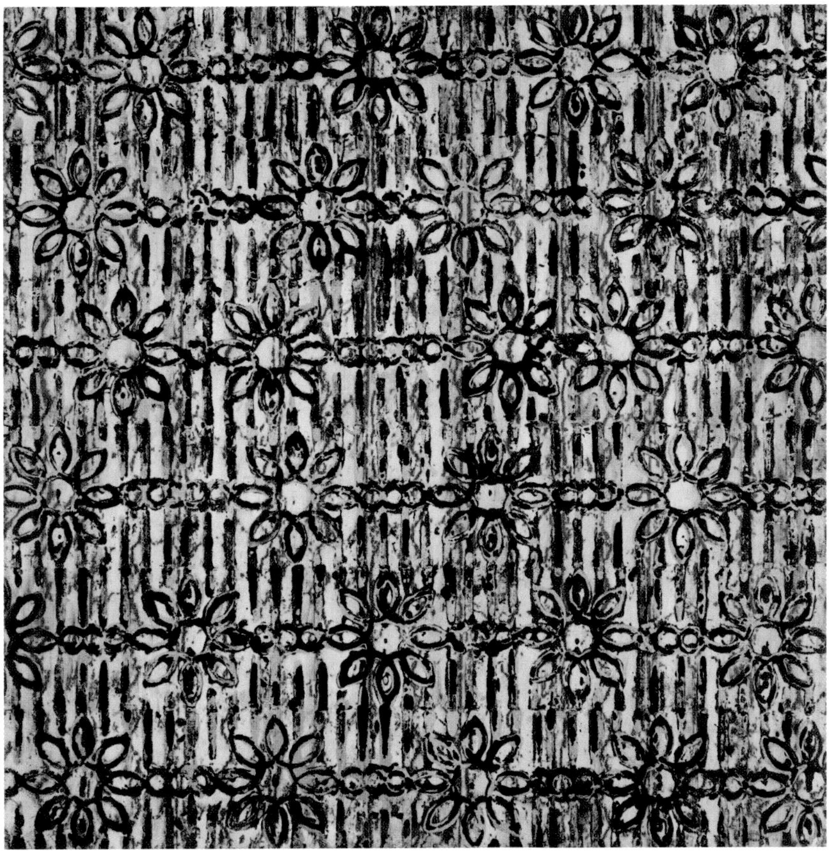

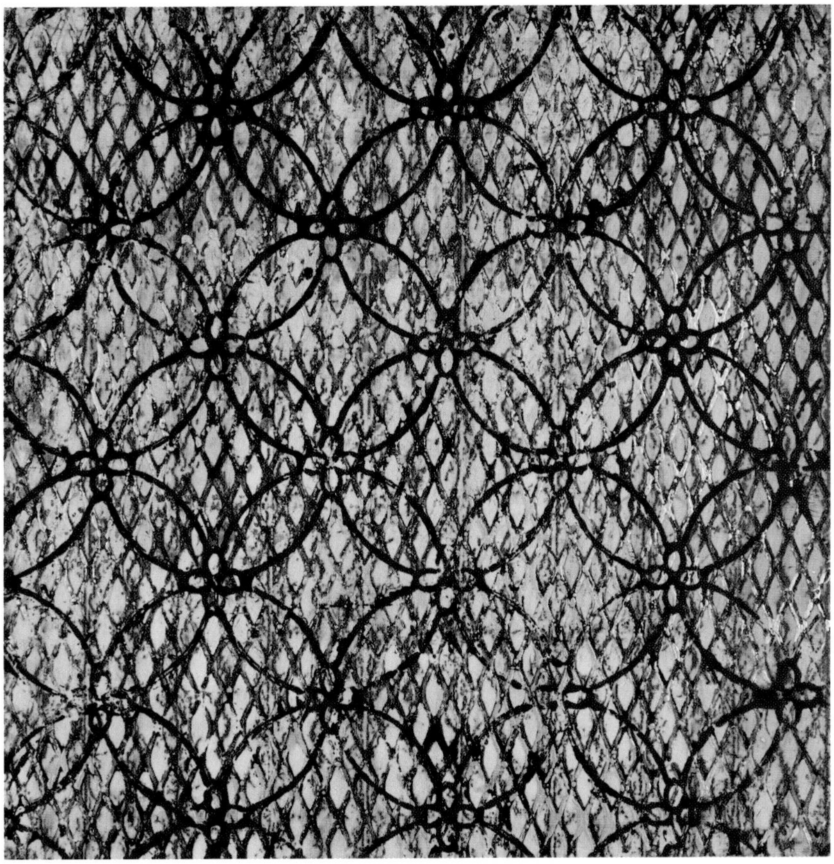

**Swoon Song**
2000
acrylic and enamel on
mylar on panel
14" x 14"

*bottom,* **BlowSpace**
1998
oil and enamel on mylar
on panel
14" x 14"
Collection of Niall Worn,
Germany

**Empire**
2010
oil and enamel on canvas
62" x 52"

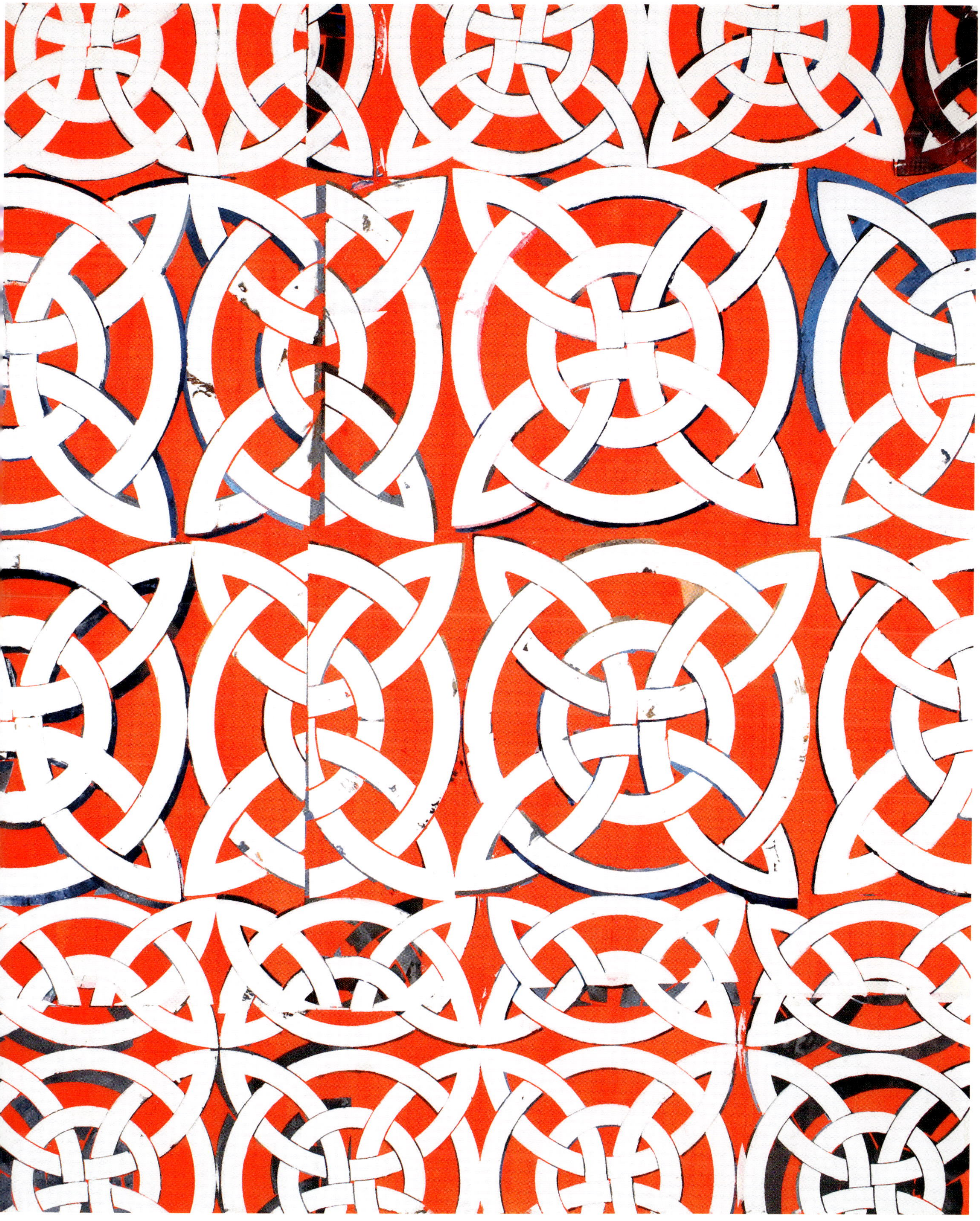

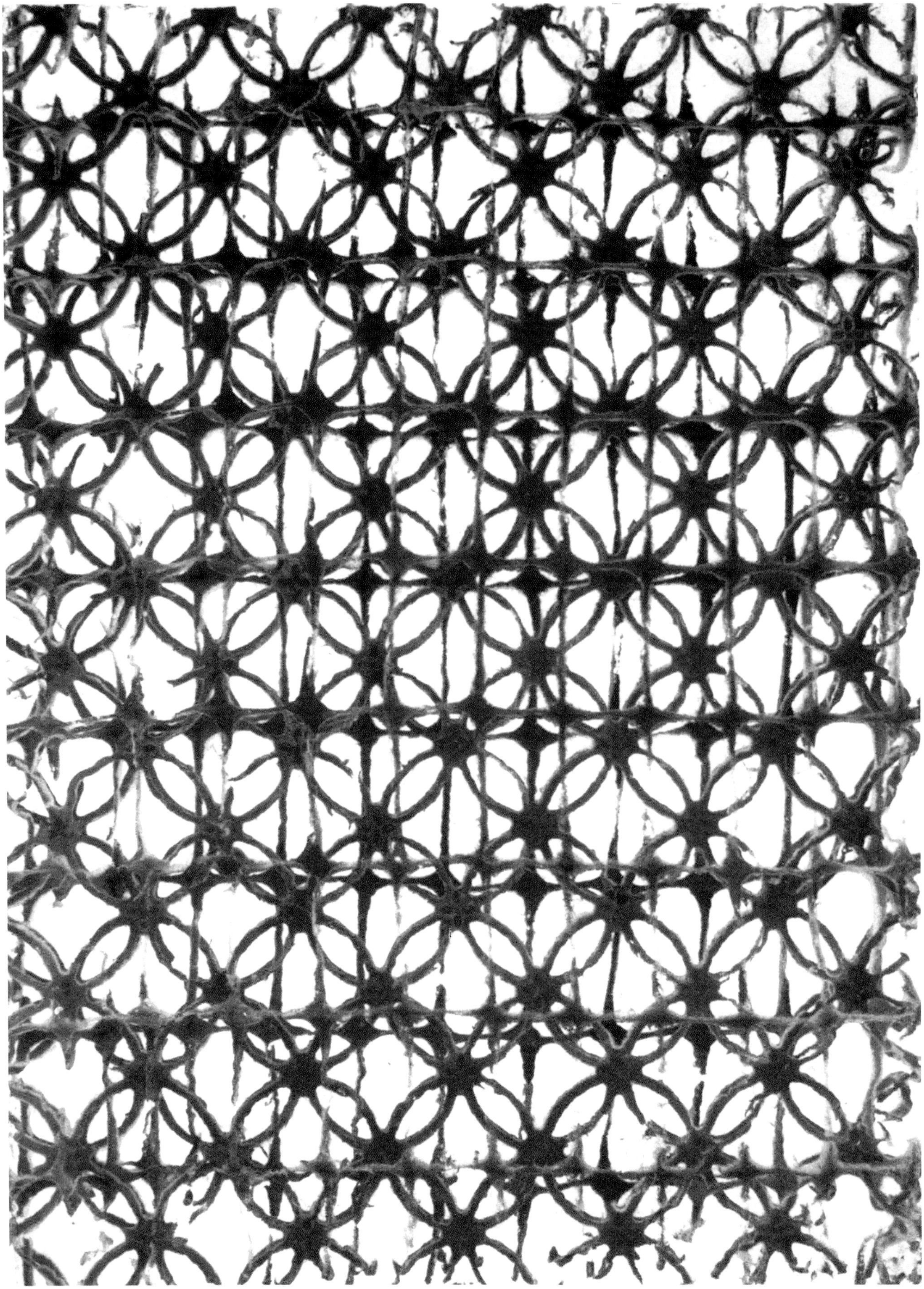

# SELECTED PUBLIC COLLECTIONS

Museum of Modern Art, New York
British Museum, London
Victoria and Albert Museum, London
The New York Public Library Print Collection
Harvard Art Museums/Fogg Museum, Cambridge
Yale University Art Gallery, New Haven
Northern Illinois University Museum, Dekalb
Cedar Rapids Museum of Art, Iowa
The Hallmark Fine Art Collection, Kansas City
Amerada Hess Corporation, New York

# SELECTED PRIVATE COLLECTIONS

Kenise Barnes, New York
Mary Kathryn Brown, Arkansas
Pamela Butler, New York
Susan Drew, Los Angeles
Bill and Jodi Gorin, New York
Dawn and Chuck Hendricks, New York
Barbara Kelly, Canada
Barbara and Roger Kohin, Worcester
Patti Kraft, Boston
Werner Kramarsky, New York
Richard Landy, New York
Leslie and Michael Meyers, New York
Jean-Yves Noblet, New York
Loan Pham, New York
Tunde and Sunder Reddy, New York
Janet and John Robinson, New York
Natasha and Ross Taylor, Australia
Nancy Tepper, New York
Bruce and Naomi Usher, New York
Dan Cullen and Chris Welch, New York
Jennifer Kroman and David Wermuth, New York
Niall Worn, Germany

*opposite,* **Black Bead Game**
1998-99
screenprinted paper pulp on cotton rag
30" x 22"
Collection of the Trustees of the British Museum

# ARTIST'S CHRONOLOGY

## EDUCATION

1977
Studio Art Center International, Florence, Italy

1978
Tyler School of Art, Rome, Italy

1979
College of the Holy Cross, Worcester, Massachusetts, cum laude BA in Fine Arts

1979-80
Parson School of Design, New York

1981
Skowhegan School of Painting and Sculpture, Maine

1989
School of Visual Arts, New York, MFA

## GRANTS AND AWARDS

1987
Graff Travel Grant, Hunter College CUNY (Guatemala)

1989
Fulbright-Hays Award (Germany)

1994
Jan Aronson and Edgar M. Bronfman Arts Program Award (co-recipient)

1996
National Endowment of the Arts-Council on Arts Fellowship

1998-99
Dieu Donne Papermill Artist's Workspace Grant

2001, 2004, 2007
MacDowell Art Colony Residency

2003
Abbey Rome Prize in Painting, British Academy, Rome

2007
**Public Art Commission**
MTA Arts For Transit New York (permanent installation of seven faceted glass panels for the Norwood subway station)

2007-2008
Fulbright Senior Research Fellowship (India and Syria)

2010
Ucross Foundation, Wyoming. Artist Residency

## EXHIBITIONS

1983
**Group Exhibitions**
The Not For Sale Show, El Bohio Gallery, New York
The Matchbook Show, Club 57, New York. curator, John Rosis
The Slow Show, The Storefront for Art and Architecture, New York. curator: Kyong Park
Color: Harmonious and Discordant, Marymount Gallery, New York. curator: Sylvia Sleigh
1000 Balloons Show, Danceteria, New York. curators: Liz and Val
The Strangers Show, Public Image Gallery, New York
Invitational, Lucky Strike Art Club, New York

**Performances**

The She-Ghost Exorcists, No Se No, New York

The Seven Days of Creation, ABC No Rio, New York

Show and Tell, The Storefront for Art and Architecture, New York

1984

**Solo Exhibition**

Fire at the Foot of the Mountain, Sakaimachi Gallery, Kyoto, Japan

**Group Exhibitions**

Exhibition: Mask!, Art Pop Communication Space, Kyoto, Japan

**Performances**

The Shinto Ghost of the Hankyu Rail, Sakaimachi Gallery, Kyoto, Japan (with Ivano Buoro)

The Gilli-Air Wind Tunnel, Lombok Island, Indonesia

1986

**Group Exhibition**

Present Intelligence, BACA Downtown, Brooklyn, New York

1987

**Group Exhibitions**

Site Specific, Thomas Hunter Gallery, New York. curator: Valerie Jaudon

R Exposition Show, COLAB, New York

Art Break Hotel, ABC No Rio, New York

1988

**Solo Exhibition**

Resonant Journeys, Visual Arts Gallery, New York

1989

**Group Exhibitions**

"line", Visual Arts Gallery, New York. curator: Loren Madsen

Cavimimaguyca: Unit/Unities, Visual Arts Gallery, New York. curator: Alan D'Arcangelo

1990

**Group Exhibitions**

Kila Mala Kola, Galerie Christa Schubbe, Mettman-Dusseldorf, Germany

Rundgang, Staatliche Kunstakademie, Dusseldorf, Germany. curator: Tony Cragg

1991

**Group Exhibitions**

Water, Trenkmann Gallery, New York

Sculpture at Chesterwood, Stockbridge, Massachusetts. curator: Linda Shearer

Future Material, Hunt's Point Sculpture Site, Bronx, New York

1992

**Group Exhibition**

Rubber Soul, LedisFlam Gallery, New York

1993

**Solo Exhibition**

Material Traces, Her Sister's Gallery, Litchfield, Connecticut

**Group Exhibitions**

Cadavre Exquis, The Drawing Center, New York

Test Wall, T'Zart Gallery, New York

Breaching Containment, Gallery Three Zero, New York

Repair Work, Deutsche Bank Gallery, New York

1994

**Solo Exhibition**

Recent Sculptures and Prints, Harlan Gallery, Seton Hill College, Pennsylvania

**Group Exhibition**

Sculpture Center Benefit Exhibition, New York

1995

**Group Exhibitions**

All-of-a-Piece, Katonah Museum, New York. curator: Robert Storr

Recycle, Re-use, Recreate. curator: Dorothy Spencer. Exhibition traveled to 14 African cities including Dakar, Accra, Lagos and Kinshasha

Doggie Style, Avene B Studio, New York. curator: Rick Prol
Behind the Eight Ball, The Police Building Gallery, New York.

1996

**Group Exhibitions**

Material Madness, The Work Space, New York. curators: Jean Wolff and Brooke Molinaroli
Permutations, The Marymount Manhattan Gallery, New York

1997

**Solo Exhibition**

New Work, Kim Foster Gallery, New York

**Group Exhibition**

Printworks, Barrett Gallery, Poughkeepsie, New York. curator: Roberta Waddell

1999

**Group Exhibition**

CRIA Benefit Exhibition, New York. organized by Ross Bleckner

2000

**Solo Exhibition**

Paper Napkin Smirk, Deborah Berke Architects, New York

**Group Exhibitions**

Six Abstract Painters, Karen McCready Fine Art, New York
Art on Paper 2000, Weatherspoon Art Museum, North Carolina
Winter Paper, Catherine Moore Gallery, New York
25th Years of Art from Dieu Donne, Milwaukee Art Museum. Exhibition traveled to Kresge Art Museum, Maryland Institute College of Art, and The Heckscher Museum of Art.
Paper Trail, Mason Gross Arts Gallery, Rutgers University, New Jersey. curators: Judith Brodsky and Andrea S. Honore

2001

**Group Exhibitions**

Remix, Dieu Donne Papermill, New York. curator: Edwin T. Ramoran, The Bronx Museum
Creativity in Western North Carolina, Hendersonville, North Carolina

2002

**Solo Exhibition**

The Strangeness of Beauty, University of Southern Maine, Portland

2003

**Group Exhibitions**

Giving Full Circle, Elizabeth Dee Gallery, New York
The Fine Arts 2002-2003, The British Academy, Rome, Italy
Methodology and Intuition, Spazio 1000, Rome, Italy

2004

**Group Exhibitions**

Queens International, The Queens Museum of Art, New York. site specific commission, curator: Hitomi Iwasaki
New Projects, Dieu Donne Papermill, New York
Prints 2004/Summer, International Print Center, New York

2005

**Group Exhibitions**

All Terrain, Average Industries Gallery, Art Basel, Miami
Private View, APT Gallery, London, UK
Plane and Form, Minnesota Center for Art, Minneapolis

2006

**Solo Exhibitions**

Plaisir, Kenise Barnes Fine Art, New York
Vapor Trail, Bernard Toale Gallery, Boston, site specific installation, Project Room

**Group Exhibitions**

Global Pop, Mills Gallery, Boston Center for the Arts. curator: Joseph Carroll
Petal Fusion, Cheryl Hazen Gallery, New York. curator: Allegra LaViola

**Art Fairs**

FLOW Miami, Kenise Barnes Fine Art, New York

2008

**Group Exhibition**

Editions/Artists Book Fair, Jean-Yves Noblet Editions, New York

2009

**Solo Exhibition**

how to live elsewhere, Kenise Barnes Fine Art, New York

**Group Exhibitions**

Fresh Asphalt, Gallery Satori, New York

RocCoPop, Dean Projects and Crossing Art Gallery, New York

2010

**Solo Exhibition**

Pet the Pretty Tiger: Works 1990-2010, Iris and B. Gerald Cantor Art Gallery, Worcester, Massachusetts. curator: Carol Schwarzman

**Group Exhibitions**

Autosemblematic, Local Projects Gallery, New York. curator: Jennifer Junkermeier

Ucross: 26 Years of Visual Art, Nicolaysen Art Museum, Wyoming. curator: Lisa Hatchadorian

**LECTURES**

1986 and 1987

The History of Japanese Gardens, The Museum of Natural History, New York, guest lecturer

1988

Gardens of the East, The Tibetan Museum, Staten Island, New York, guest lecturer

1993-1994

The Isamu Noguchi Museum, Long Island City, staff lecturer

1995

Harlan Gallery, Seton Hill College, Greensburg, Pennsylvania, visiting artist

2000, 01

Western Carolina University, visiting artist, BFA program

2002

University of Southern Maine, Artist-in-Residence

Mount Holyoke College, Massachusetts, visiting artist

2005

Western Carolina University, visiting artist, MFA program

Asheville Museum of Art, North Carolina, guest lecturer

2006

Makor-Steinhardt Center, New York, "Beauty's Burden" panel discussion, moderator: David Gibson

2008

University of Baroda, India, visiting artist

Institute of Art and Design, Jaipur, India, visiting artist

2010

College of the Holy Cross, Massachusetts, visiting artist

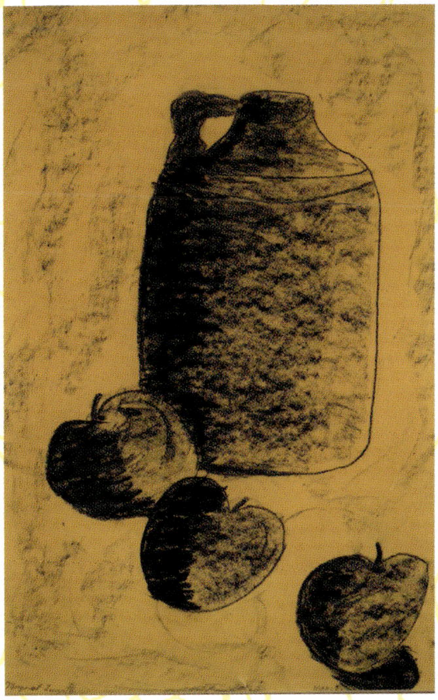

**Still Life with Apples**
1963
charcoal on construction paper
17" x 11"

# BIBLIOGRAPHY


## BOOKS

2010

*Pet the Pretty Tiger: Works 1990-2010*, essays by John Yau and Judy Halebsky

2002

*Unframed, Artists' Respond to AIDS*, forward by Manuel Gonzalez

2006

*Prints Now, Directions and Definitions*, Gill Saunders and Rosemary Miles, Victoria and Albert Museum Publications, United Kingdom

## EXHIBITION CATALOGUES

1991

*Contemporary Sculpture at Chesterwood*, by Linda Shearer

1993

*Breaching Containment*, by Tom Zollner, Gallery Three Zero, New York

1995

*Recycle, Re-use, Recreate*, by Dorothy Spencer, curator

*Permutations*, by Karen L. Harris, director, MMC Gallery, New York

1996

*Material Madness*, by Jeff Howe

2000

*paperTrail*, by Judith Brodsky and Andrea S. Honore

*Art on Paper 2000*, by Nancy Doll, curator, Weatherspoon Art Museum

2001

*Creativity in Western North Carolina*, by Dian Magie

*Remix*, by Edwin T. Ramoran, curator, The Bronx Museum

2003

*The Fine Arts 2002-2003*, The British Academy, Rome, Italy

2004

*Queens International*, essay by Hitomi Iwasaki, curator, The Queens Museum of Art

2010

*Autosemblematic*, essay by Jennifer Junkermeier

## ARTICLES/REVIEWS

1983

The Village Voice, Illustration, March 29

1984

*The Kansai Art Review*, Television Interview, KBS Network, Kyoto, Japan

*American Sculptor in Japan*, Republic American, David Boraks, April 15

*Fire at the Foot of the Mountain*, Kansai Time Out, Osaka, Japan. March, Vol. No. 85

*A New Look at Sculpture*, The Kyoto Symbol News, Yasu Kode. Illustration, May 7

*Sculptural Intimations*, Ikebana Ohara Journal, Osaka, Japan, Totsui Otsah. Illustration: 3 sculptures. May, Vol. No. 402

1986

*Baca's Version of "Intelligence"*, The Phoenix, Barbara Belejak, Brooklyn, New York, May 19

1995

*"All-of-a-Piece"*, The New York Times, William Zimmerman, June 11

2000

"Six Abstract Painters", The New York Times, Ken Johnson. July 29

"Margaret Lanzetta at Deborah Berke Architects", Zingmagazine, Carol Schwarzman

2003

*Collecting the Contemporary*, Gill Saunders, Victoria and Albert Museum Art Journal United Kingdom

*Cosi La Mostra*, La Republica, Rome, Mario de Candia, June 20

2006

*Vapor Trail at Bernard Toale Gallery*, Hand Papermaking Journal, Mina Takahashi, ed.,

*Global Pop: We ARE What We Buy*, Boston Globe, Cate McQuaid, October 12

*Global Pop: We ARE What We Buy*, South End News, Dan Peleschuk, October 19

*Plane and Form at Minnesota Center for Arts*, Hand Papermaking Journal, Kay Searle.

2007

*Finding Patterns*, Republican American, Tracey O'Shaughnessy, November 13

2010

*Pattern Repetition*, Worcester Magazine, Larry Levey, October


Artist's garden, winter, Long Island City 2010

*overleaf*, Artist's garden, summer, Long Island City 2010

# ACKNOWLEDGMENTS

I am eternally grateful to my husband, David Packer, for his support, help and encouragement, and especially for his patience during the two years of planning this exhibition. Special thanks also go to dear friends who have championed my work over the years and who were invaluable in making this exhibition and catalogue possible: Kenise Barnes, Pam Butler, the late Jim Fulop, Leslie Gerber-Seid, Pita Kelekna, Kevin Noble, Bruce Richards, Niall Worn and Roger Hankins and the Holy Cross Community. I am immensely grateful to Chris Welch for her long friendship and the design of this most wonderful catalogue and to Judy Halebsky, Carol Schwarzman and John Yau for their insightful essays. Thank you to all the individuals and museum institutions who have also supported my work; it is an honor to be in your collections. Long periods of creativity and incredible inspiration have been possible with support from The Fulbright Commission, The National Endowment for the Arts, the MacDowell Art Colony, the Ucross Foundation, The British Academy in Rome, Dieu Donne Papermill and the Skowhegan School. I am deeply grateful to my past teachers for their passion and guidance, in particular the late Barbara Schwartz, and to Jackie Haught for her wisdom and healing. Finally, I thank my parents for encouraging me to be an artist from the very beginning.

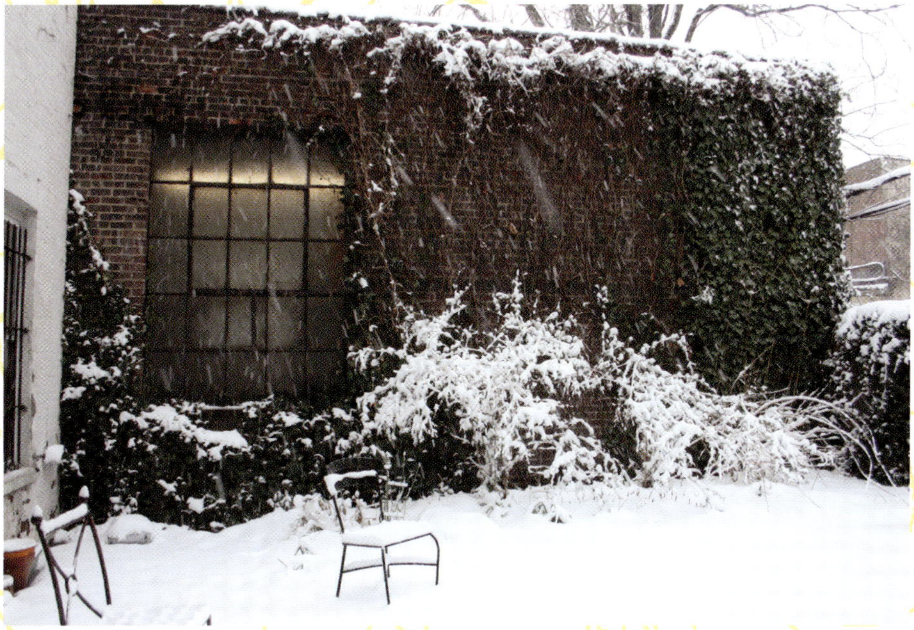

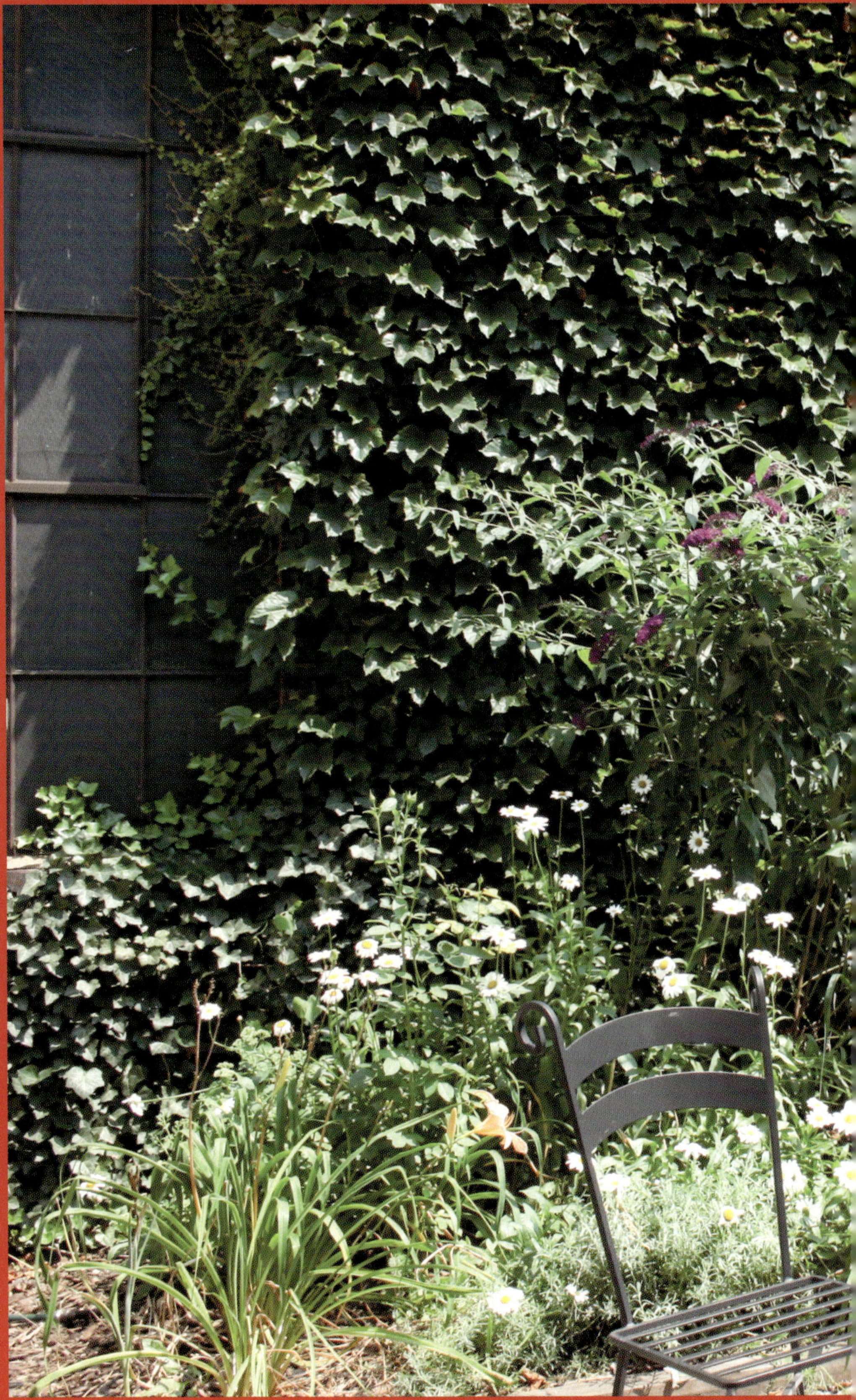

Printed in edition of 1,000 at Linco Printing
Inc., Long Island City, New York